Teaching Creative Arts and Media 14+

sity Campus

University Centre Barnsley

University of
HUDDERSFIELD

Renewals: 01226 644281

Renewals: 01484 472045 (24hrs)

UniversityCentre
Barnsley

Class No: 302·230712

Suffix: MAY

This book is to be returned on or before
the last date stamped below

Teaching 14+

Series editor: Andy Armitage

Published titles:

Teaching Creative Arts and Media 14+

Markham May and Sue Warr

Open University Press

Open University Press
McGraw-Hill Education
McGraw-Hill House
Shoppenhangers Road
Maidenhead
Berkshire
England
SL6 2QL

email: enquiries@openup.co.uk
world wide web: www.openup.co.uk

and Two Penn Plaza, New York, NY 10121-2289, USA

First published 2011

Copyright © Markham May and Sue Warr 2011

A catalogue record of this book is available from the British Library

ISBN-13: 978-0-33-523752-4 (pb) 978-0-33-523751-7 (hb)
ISBN-10: 0-33-523752-5 (pb) 0-33-523751-7 (hb)
eISBN: 978-0-33-523997-9

Library of Congress Cataloging-in-Publication Data
CIP data applied for

Typeset by RefineCatch Limited, Bungay, Suffolk
Printed in the UK by CPI Antony Rowe, Chippenham and Eastbourne

Fictitious names of companies, products, people, characters and/or data that
may be used herein (in case studies or in examples) are not intended to
represent any real individual, company, product or event.

The *McGraw·Hill* Companies

Contents

List of figures, tables and boxes

Figures

Tables

Boxes

Series editor's preface

For historical reasons perhaps, subject pedagogy for post-16 teachers has not been considered a professional development priority. The possession of appropriate academic or vocational qualifications and experience has traditionally been considered sufficient for those teaching older students who are assumed themselves to possess the motivation and skills for effective learning. However, the increasing numbers of 14–16 year olds taking part in their programmes in further education (FE) colleges, the rise in the participation rate of 16–19 year olds and the increasing number of 18–30 year olds having experience of higher education, all have created a large and diverse population in all sector institutions presenting a challenge to those teaching post-14 students. Both the 2003 and 2006 Ofsted surveys of post-16 teacher training and the 2007 reforms of initial teacher training and continuing professional development, have drawn attention to the urgent need for both new and existing teachers to receive training to teach their subject or curriculum specialism and to receive support from subject coaches or mentors in the workplace. Most of the programmes preparing the 40,000 trainees annually to teach in the lifelong learning sector are generic in nature, rather than subject specific.

Partly because of the Institute for Learning's requirements regarding both continuing professional development (CPD) and professional formation, there is considerable growth in in-service CPD and, given the attention by both Ofsted and the Department for Education to subject pedagogy as described above, it is likely that there will be a sharp CPD focus for many colleges on subject teaching, particularly since much of the burden of subject based training will fall on the shoulders of FE college based mentors. The increase in vocational education in schools, particularly with the introduction of Diplomas, will see a growing need for secondary postgraduate certificate in education (PGCE) students and existing 14–18 secondary teachers to enhance their subject pedagogy for 14+ students. One of the key recommendations of a report in 2010 on vocational teacher training is that 'Vocational and applied pedagogies should become a research priority and be embedded within school, further education (FE) and higher education (HE) initial teacher training (ITT) and continuing professional development (CPD).'[1]

Each series title is therefore aimed to act as support for teachers, whether on a formal initial or CPD programme, or simply as a guide for those teaching the subject on a daily basis in one of a variety of possible contexts: secondary, FE, adult and community education, work-based training. Chapters in each title follow a similar format. Chapter 1 deals with the nature of subject(s) in the curriculum area, considering any contesting conceptions of what the subject should be about, as well as current issues connected with teaching it. There is a focus on subject updating, identifying recent key developments in subjects as well as the means for students to be able to update themselves. Chapter 2 provides an introduction to the major programmes in the subject area focusing mainly on those in the National Qualifications Framework such as General Certificate of Secondary Education (GCSE), Advanced Subsidiary (AS), Key Skills, National Vocational Qualification (NVQ), Diplomas, although reference is made to the Framework for Higher Education Qualifications and the forthcoming Qualification and Credit Framework. There is a consideration of the central features of each programme such as aims and objectives, unitization or modularity, content. The chapter also guides readers in the task of turning syllabus into learning via schemes of work. The third and fourth chapters are concerned with skills: employability and life skills, key skills and functional skills, wider key skills, business and enterprise, research, team building and project management skills. It looks at differing models of skills development and how such skills might be taught through the subject. Chapter 5 looks at the teaching and learning strategies most often used in the curriculum area. There are clearly certain learning and teaching strategies that are used universally across post-14 programmes – lectures, discussion, presentations are the most obvious. Even these, however, will need to be treated in the context of their use in the subject area. Presentations which model those in advertising or marketing might be effective learning strategies in an AS Media Studies or Applied Business GCSE, whereas in Key Skills Communications they might have the purpose of developing oracy skills and as part of an access course of developing study skills. Chapter 6 considers resources as used in the context of the curriculum area. When audio-visual resources are being considered, for example, students might be presented with exemplar handouts and PowerPoint presentations with subject-related content. Information and communication technology (ICT) resources should be considered in terms of their strengths in relation to the subject. Are there good commercial software packages, for example? How can they best be used for teaching? What are the key websites relating to the subject area? How might searching best be carried out? There is a consideration of the range of published resources available in the subject area, with examples of how material is presented and how use of it is structured. Chapter 7 offers guidance on the role of the teacher as assessor in the programmes identified in Chapter 2, with a particular emphasis on the range of assessment strategies used as part of these programmes.

Each title features a range of pedagogical features which might be useful alone, in pairs or in groups. Readers are invited for example to reflect, discuss, respond to a range of visual stimuli, give short answer responses to questions, consider case studies and complete short tasks.

Markham May and Sue Warr note the complexity of the arts and media sector as a whole and it follows that the task of preparing students to enter that sector will be equally complex. Furthermore, creative arts and media subjects have a range of both vocational and non-vocational ends, as do the students who take them and May and Warr's accomplishment is that they have provided such comprehensive detailed guidance for their teachers. Many teachers will have relatively narrow subject specialisms and the increasing challenge of the developing 14–19 curriculum is that it demands a broader skills base for those who teach it. So the English teacher, the drama teacher, for example, will find excellent links throughout the book between the key specialisms in creative arts and media. Both May and Warr have many years' experience working with both students and teachers and this experience shows on every page. And it is appropriate that, for a text concerned with creativity, the authors demonstrate such liveliness and originality in every aspect of their work: from the striking examples and illustrations to the novel, stimulating pedagogical features.

Andy Armitage – Series Editor

Reference

1   Skills Commission (2010) *An Inquiry into Teacher Training in Vocational Education.* London: Skills Commission p.14

Preface

Why read this book?

Creative arts and media programmes have proliferated in recent years. There has been much innovative teaching to learners who have produced inspiring, high quality work. However, the very popularity of the programmes for learners and the complexity, size and dynamic nature of the sector provides great challenges for teachers. There is also a need to persuade not only learners but also others such as parents or employers that creative arts and media programmes are demanding and relevant for success in life and work. This book intends to explore such challenges and offer guidance and ideas on how to make creative arts and media teaching relevant, stimulating and above all creative!

Teaching and learning in the twenty-first century for all subject areas needs to respond to the economic and cultural changes in society and the increased demands of employers for transferable skills. The characteristics and needs of learners growing up in a sophisticated digital and competitive world require fresh teaching approaches in order to motivate and develop learners' knowledge and skills.

What is meant by creative arts and media?

The Ofsted Inspection Framework refers sometimes to arts, media and publishing. Recent developments in education have introduced a new name, creative arts and media. However, this book is not linked to any specific qualification or programme of learning. *Teaching Creative Arts and Media 14+* covers three main areas – media, art and design, and performing arts. These disciplines are often interlinked and increasingly there is a need for teachers and learners to appreciate the connections between subjects that only a few years ago would have been considered, particularly in schools, as very separate areas.

Within the book, we refer to creative arts and media when referring to programmes of learning, qualifications and learners. However, for simplicity, we sometimes refer to creative and media industries and creative professionals, with the implication that these cover all three disciplines.

Who is this book for?

The book is aimed primarily at teachers or those training to be teachers in all of the various organizations that are involved in delivering the 14–19 curriculum. This includes schools, sixth forms, further education colleges, work-based learning organizations, adult and community learning, the secure estates and pupil referral units. Many other organizations and individuals are getting involved in the exciting landscape that is 14–19 education and we hope that this book may also be useful for the industry experts, employers and others who are increasingly coming into contact with learners and who want to understand more about creative arts and media education.

You may be from an industry background, new to teaching and wish to extend your knowledge of appropriate teaching and learning approaches, or you may be an experienced teacher who has delivered so-called 'academic' qualifications in, for instance, English or film studies and now wish to extend your teaching or gain confidence in more 'vocational' areas.

How can this book help my professional development?

This book supports your continuing professional development (CPD) as each chapter requires you to reflect on your practice and plan further actions in relation to your teaching of creative arts and media 14+.

This is not a textbook giving information about specific creative and media businesses, equipment or techniques but it is about giving you approaches and strategies which will enable you to sustain your own creativity, inspiration and engagement in an area where young people are often prime consumers and expert users of creative products, services and performances.

Whatever your background and motivation, 'Welcome!' We hope that you find the following pages interesting and stimulating.

Markham May
Sue Warr

Acknowledgements

Over the years we have visited hundreds of educational organizations delivering crea-tive arts and media programmes and met many inspirational teachers, managers and support staff. This book is based on our experiences of working in the sector and in particular our observations of learning sessions and assessment of learner evidence.

This book would not have been written without the support and advice of our colleagues within the teaching profession with whom we have worked and who have shared their thoughts, ideas, successes and concerns with us.

We would particularly like to mention the organizations whose learners appear in the photographs on the front cover:

- The Valance School
- North Warwickshire and Hinckley College
- Access to Music

Thanks to Fiona Richman, editor, and Stephanie Frosch, editorial assistant at Open University Press, for their support. We are also grateful to Andy Armitage, series editor, for his advice and encouragement.

We would like to thank our families for their forbearance during the writing of this book.

Markham May
Sue Warr

1

The creative arts and media world

Features and processes

By the end of this chapter, you will be able to:

- Explain what is meant by creativity and the creative arts and media processes
- Understand the attributes of creative people and the relevance of creative arts and media skills for employment and life
- Recognize the scope and importance of the creative arts and media sector

---

Introduction

The 'creative arts' can be considered to be about the generation and development of concepts and ideas and 'media' about the format and way in which concepts and ideas are recorded and transmitted. This opening chapter explores what creativity and the media really mean for teachers and learners and how creative arts and media processes and skills can be transferable.

There is a section on the attributes of creative people, their personal qualities and skills and whether creativity is a natural talent or something that can be learned. We refer to the value of creative arts and media skills in other areas.

The final section looks at the different areas within the creative and media industries and the interrelationship between them and other sectors. The creative and media sector is an important contributor to the UK economy and there is a focus on the role of the sector skills councils in developing a creative workforce in collaboration with educational organizations and employers.

What is creativity?

Creativity is essentially a thought process, the ability to perceive and work with abstract concepts or with concrete realities in new or different ways. This thought process can initiate language, visuals, movement, sound, smell or a combination of these. Creativity implies change. Words that are frequently associated with creativity include 'new', 'original', 'fresh', 'daring', 'world changing', 'inventive', 'resourceful', 'transformational', 'disruptive', 'challenging', 'inspired' and 'unconventional'.

Creativity is about choosing a direction or focus, selecting materials, and making decisions: not just doing or replicating. In creativity, there is a sense of purpose: of making a difference. So in essence, the media person and the creative person can be two sides of the same coin. An editor or a journalist, a reporter of the 'truth' can be a creative person as much as the science fiction writer or the abstract artist. Conversely, the musician composing popular songs to upload onto the Internet uses media skills.

People can place different values on different types of creative activity, just as some people might differentiate between 'high art' and 'popular art'. The purest type of art is sometimes seen as one that transcends words and directly affects the emotions and intellect such as a classical symphony. In comparison, popular dance music might be considered a lesser form because it stimulates movement rather than profound thought. It is interesting how people may value different creative forms. The German philosopher Friedrich von Schelling saw architecture as frozen music (*gefrorener Musik*) and it has been argued that all art forms are based on the principles of music (fleeting, emotional and subjective) and architecture (lasting, spatial and objective).

Goethe was one of the greatest poets yet his character Faust's heroic aim is to 'perceive the innermost working of things and not to rummage around in words' ('Schau alle Wirkenskraft und Samen und tu nicht mehr in Worten kramen'). Why is this of interest to the creative arts and media teacher?

There is a danger that vocational creative arts and media courses are devalued because of the public perception (sometimes fuelled by the newspapers) that they focus on popular and more ephemeral products such as magazines and television soaps whereas 'academic' qualifications focus on classical or 'great' creative works such as opera or Shakespeare plays which are perceived to be 'harder' and more worthwhile.

Reflection 1.1

- Can creativity be solely a thought process or does there need to be a physical, end product that can be appreciated by human senses?
- Are creative arts and media programmes seen as a soft option because celebrity culture and the media portray success in the creative and media industries as being either through luck or 'who you know'?

What is the creative process?

The creative process, similar to the communication process, often requires a receiver or end user: in other words, an audience, reader, viewer, listener, games player, consumer. As in the communication process, these people may not be passive users; they can also be part of the creative process (see Figures 1.1 and 1.2).

Geoff Petty defines the creative process as consisting of 'six working phases, *inspiration, clarification, distillation, perspiration, evaluation, and incubation*. During a

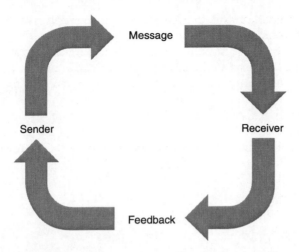

Figure 1.1 The communication process

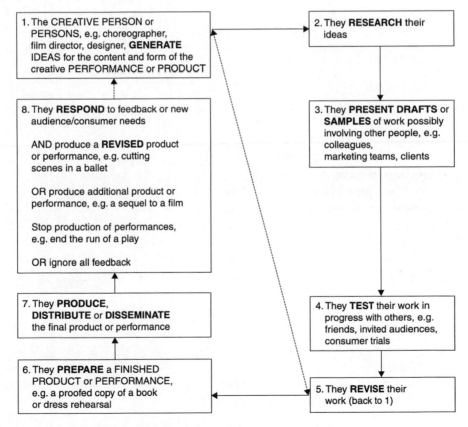

Figure 1.2 Communication and the creative process

particular piece of creative work each phase should be experienced many times, in no definite order, sometimes for a very short time.'[1]

The creative process is not a linear one. The starting point will depend on the context and who is involved in the creative process. So it may or may not start with the generation of ideas. For example, a camera operator may test camera angles for a director and then come up with ideas to make a shot that has greater impact or meaning. A newspaper subeditor may refine a news story but may then suggest new ideas to the journalist to include in the story. A computer games designer might try out existing games with a potential new market before generating ideas for a new game.

Reflection 1.2

Look at the following list of activities. Place them in order with the most creatively demanding at the top and the least creatively demanding at the bottom. You will need to decide on the criteria on which you will base your decisions such as the length of time needed by the creative person or the demands of an audience or value of the work. For those activities that you rate as least creative, think about what might make them more creative.

These activities are all based around the written word, but you could adapt them to relate to dance, music, art, filmmaking, acting or even areas such as engineering or marketing. This activity is best carried out with a group of people so that you can compare and discuss responses.

- Writing a poem for a women's magazine
- Writing a news story for the local paper
- Writing advertising copy for a new car
- Writing a play on a social issue
- Writing a comedy script for commercial radio
- Making up a joke for young children
- Writing a letter to the editor of a newspaper
- Writing an entertaining novel for adults
- Reading a poem to a group of teenagers
- Reading radio news on hospital radio
- Acting a role in a television advertisement
- Acting a minor role in a serious play
- Telling a joke to a colleague at work
- Reading a magazine article to learners
- Reading an entertaining novel on holiday
- Editing news stories for a national newspaper
- Adapting an entertaining novel for radio
- Translating a novel into another language
- Writing a review of a play for a magazine.

What is meant by media and mediation?

The media were traditionally thought of as:

- Print – newspapers and magazines, books, photography
- Audio – radio and recorded music
- Audio-visual – video production, film and television.

Then towards the end of the twentieth century came an addition:

- Multimedia – web pages, computer games, the linking of a range of media together including the visual and the performing arts.

Most media products have the potential for mass communication. This is the transmission of information or ideas from either one person or a group of people to a large group of people. How this is done will depend on the industry. A novel such as J.K. Rowling's *Harry Potter and the Order of the Phoenix* was first issued in the traditional form of a printed book.[2] In this format, a fictional story about imaginary events thought up by one woman was transmitted around the world to millions of readers. This is an example of single authorship. In comparison, regional radio news from a station such as Mercia FM is broadcast to thousands of listeners. It tells of real events, people and places. It is an example of multiple authorship in that many people including the journalists, the presenter, guests, sometimes the public and the radio editor will have all made significant contributions to the end product.

The performing arts, in conjunction with the media, can also be part of this mass communication. The music industry combines both performing arts and media in the transmission of performances around the world through television and radios, sales of compact discs (CDs) and downloads from the Internet. Neither now, need the audiences for live theatre performances be limited by the seating capacity of a venue. Live streaming of performances over the Internet is increasing.

Mediation takes place when ideas or events are turned into 'messages' and distributed to audiences and consumers (either in the form of media products, works of art or performances). These messages are mediated by the following:

- The interpretation placed on them by writers (or camera operators, artists, composers, choreographers)
- The decisions of editors, producers and clients
- The nature of the medium, for example print publication, television, theatre, gallery
- The demands of the marketplace
- Their reception by the different audiences or consumers.

> **Reflection 1.3**
>
> Read the following example of mediation and reflect on how performances or works of art might be affected by similar influences. Think also how learners' work is 'mediated' when they work on group projects.
>
> > A Russian journalist writes about a terrorist attack on the Moscow Underground. The report is translated and sent to an international news agency. The story is bought by a European tabloid. The Western news editor concentrates on the human rather than the political angle and cuts the number of words. A photograph is included with the article showing an injured child. A major figure in British politics dies and the article is shortened and moved from the front page to page 4. There is a heavy snowfall on the day the story is published.

Attributes and skills of creative people

The creative person will be imaginative, reflective, enterprising, flexible; an individual who can take intellectual risks. How do you become creative? Consider the two following questions that are of great importance for creative arts and media teachers:

* Is creativity an attribute that some people are born with?
* Can creativity be taught?

Theories

The research of Roger Sperry and his associates suggested that the brain houses two separate realms of consciousness.[3] Since Sperry's original research in 1981, there has been much discussion as to which side of the brain houses the area that is responsible for creativity. Some research suggests that as some people use the side of the brain 'responsible for creativity' more than the other. These people are perceived as being more creative. Some research points to the idea that in a right-handed person, the left part of the brain covers logical, analytical, objective thinking sometimes called critical thinking. The right side of the brain covers subjective, intuitive, emotional and holistic thinking. This is the side that is considered the 'creative' side of the brain. The theory tends to support those who think that creativity is a 'natural talent' or a 'gift'.

However, this division of left and right brain skills may be too simplistic. More recent research by Centre for Educational Research and Innovation (CERI) combining neuroscience, psychology and learning indicates that mathematical abilities, for example, are distributed in several parts of the brain.[4] A conclusion reached from this research is that the complex way in which the brain works, means that teachers need to use different processes to teach numbers. The same may be true for learning other knowledge and skills.

In November 2009, Stuart Jefferies, a journalist, wrote about an experiment run by Professor Sophie Scott, a psychologist, in which Fiona Shaw, an actor, underwent a brain scan.[5] During the scan, Fiona Shaw alternated counting a series of numbers with reciting the poetry of T.S. Eliot, in which she portrayed contrasting roles. The results showed that the actor used more brain areas when reciting the poetry, including a section of the brain connected with visualization, than when reciting the numbers. Interestingly, this part of the brain was not used when non-professional actors spoke in a different accent.

Lateral thinking

No consideration about creativity could omit the work of Edward de Bono.[6] He has been influential in helping people to think differently and find new approaches to solving problems. De Bono's view of creativity is that it is not a mystical gift but a learnable skill. We make assumptions all the time about the world around us and often accept too quickly our first response or solution to a challenge or problem. Lateral thinking is about changing these assumptions, which in turn affects our thinking, our perceptions and our approaches to solving problems.

Relevance of creative arts and media skills for employment and life

The world around us is changing fast. This is a compelling reason why we need to help our learners to become creative, innovative thinkers who can challenge norms and conventional wisdom who can find new solutions to new and age-old problems. If we consider creativity in this context, the debate changes from 'Can creativity be taught?' to 'How do we continue to survive and prosper if we cannot adapt?'

Working in other sectors

Learners may not be on a creative arts and media course because they want employment within the sector. They may 'like film' or 'want to be able to play the guitar'. Dance or design may not be their main focus; it might be just a subject that they prefer to take rather than a science subject or a language. Nevertheless, it may be the spark that enables them to engage with the learning process and therefore learn more effectively. They will acquire transferable skills that they can use in many jobs (see Chapters 3 and 4).

It is worth noting here, the significant relationships between many creative and non-creative industries. For instance:

- Retail and advertising
- Tourism and the theatre
- Art and the built environment
- Politics and the media
- Hospitality and music.

Multiskilling

Changes in technology and working practices and downsizing of companies have led to an expectation that employees in the creative industries will be able to multiskill.

News journalists need to be able to write their reports, set up equipment, speak to camera, edit the news package within tight timescales and pitch it against other packages competing for precious airtime. Musicians need to be able to write, produce and perform their own music as well as market themselves, manage their own tours and handle their business.

Reflection 1.4

Table 1.1 lists famous people who can multiskill. Their primary roles (what they are best known for) are indicated in the third column. Other areas in which they are skilled are in the right-hand column. Table 1.1 could be cut up to make a matching card sort for learners. Learners could be asked to research the answers and also add to the list. This could also form the basis of a quiz. Learners might wish to debate the skills of celebrities such as the two at the bottom of the list. Learners could also be asked to identify these people's specialist skills and transferable skills.

Table 1.1 Famous people with specialist and transferable skills

Famous person	Date of birth	Primary role	Secondary role
Mikhail Baryshnikov	1948	Ballet dancer	Actor
Floella Benjamin	1949	Actor/presenter	Writer
Paloma Picasso	1949	Jewellery and fashion designer	Fragrance designer/ business woman
Ai Weiwei	1957	Artist/architectural designer	Blogger/social activist
Madonna	1958	Singer	Author
Ben Elton	1959	Comedian	Novelist
Nigella Lawson	1960	Food writer	Journalist/ broadcaster
Mat Fraser	1962	Drummer	Actor/presenter
Salma Hayek	1966	Actor	Television producer/ director
Tanni Grey-Thompson	1969	Paralympic champion	Campaigner/ broadcaster
Nigel Barker	1972	Fashion photographer	Model/television judge
Peter Andre	1973	Singer/songwriter	Television personality
Victoria Beckham	1974	Singer	Fashion designer

The value of creativity in everyday life

The benefit of creative arts and media skills is not only in relation to employment. The appreciation and practice of music, art, drama, filming, reading and writing substantially enhance the individual's personal life. Music, for example, can contribute to both mental and physical well-being. It can be used not only as entertainment but also as therapy. It can be a solitary pursuit (listening to an iPod) or a group activity (playing with other musicians). It can be relaxing but it can also be invigorating and motivational.

Reflection 1.5

Think about your personal creativity:

- How important is creativity to you as a person?
- If you had to express your creativity, how would you do it? Through sound? Through movement? Through words or through making a mark? Or are you primarily a creative thinker?
- How much creative thought or action is part of your average day?
- How much is creativity an essential ingredient in your teaching?

The scope and importance of the creative arts and media sector

The creative arts and media sector covers three main categories or disciplines that provide products, performances and services for consumers and audiences:

- Performing arts
- Art and design
- Media.

Within these broad areas can be found a wide range of industries, some of which are well established and some new. For example, media not only cover television and film but also include the rapidly expanding computer games industry. Teachers can feel challenged by the rise of new genres. For example, grime, garage, bassline, dubstep, UK garage, hip hop and indie have emerged as forms of urban music; some music teachers may feel that lack of knowledge, skills and the vocabulary of this area may erode their status as 'music experts' within the learning situation.

The interrelationship between creative arts and media disciplines

Many learning programmes or qualifications are based on recognized disciplines and teachers are often experts within one of these areas. This can lead to learners narrowing their experience at an early stage. The reality of the creative and media world is that there are strong interrelationships between the three main disciplines of visual arts, performing arts and the media. The film editor needs to know about marketing and advertising in order to make a successful cinema trailer. The choreographer needs an understanding of costume design and the properties of the material used to clothe the performers in the dance. The visual artist may wish to use sound to enhance their work in an exhibition, which may be a multimedia-based art form that incorporates all three disciplines. What interlinks all of the arts is the way that artists respond to stimuli and their creative responses involve processes that are common, irrespective of the art form that is being created.

Reflection 1.6

There are many ways of understanding the interrelationships that exist within and across the differing disciplines. The hierarchy diagram (Figure 1.3) indicates a narrowing pathway approach. You might use this with learners as a starting point in investigating their aspirations or in their understanding of a discipline or subset of roles within a particular aspect of the industry.

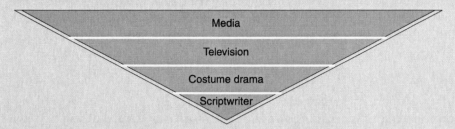

Figure 1.3 Hierarchical diagram of a creative pathway

You might find it useful to give learners a different template, such as the radial or spider diagram (Figure 1.4). This could be used to test existing knowledge or information or as a way of linking research on a particular aspect of creative and media. This is useful to help learners see the relationship between different elements of a topic or discipline.

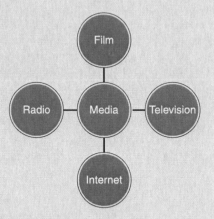

Figure 1.4 Radial diagram showing links between creative areas

Using a converging diagram (Figure 1.5) can help learners to think about the strong interrelationships between the performing arts, art and design, and media. Completing this diagram could help learners to think about the wide range of knowledge they might need in their life and work and also the similarity and differences of skill sets within different elements of their work and creative disciplines.

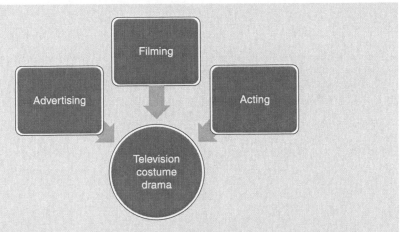

Figure 1.5 Diagram showing convergence of disciplines within a creative area

Reflection 1.7

In the review of the dance performance below, different creative arts and media areas are highlighted. In reading the review, consider the depth and breadth of knowledge that the choreographer needed in these areas. How do you think he acquired his knowledge, through general life experience, personal research or through collaboration with experts in other areas?

Matthew Bourne's *Dorian Gray* was performed on the 17th September 2009 at The Curve Theatre in Leicester. . . . This contemporary **dance** performance was based on a 19th century classic. The production takes the story of Oscar Wilde's **novel** *The Picture of Dorian Gray* and transfers it to a 21st century setting in which Dorian is seduced by the world of **advertising** and the celebrity culture of **reality television**. Many of the icons of that culture are present, the **paparazzi**, the **night-club** with its glitter ball, the alcohol fuelled partying. The lead character with his shaven head and boxer shorts, who models aftershave, is reminiscent of David Beckham and the **brands** he represents.

The performance seems closer to a **multimedia** production than to traditional **ballet** and this surely contributed to its appeal to the many younger members of the audience. The moving circular stage enables rapid changes of scene like those in a **TV soap**. The **acting**, **music**, **lighting**, **scenery** and the **photography** displayed on a **screen** overhead are key elements and contribute to the fascination of this **performance**. The **dancing** whether in an **ensemble** or in the solos was of a high quality showing sensitivity and precision.

The audience feels a range of emotions; admiration of the lead's beauty and his material success, and the **electronic music** in particular illustrates the passion and excitement of Dorian's world. The restrained black and white **costumes** express the sophisticated yet almost clinical atmosphere of a **media** world, which creates its own heroes and villains.

There are **humorous** touches: the glitter ball that is actually a **Damien Hirst style diamond skull**, the lovers revealed hiding under Damien's sheets; there are

musical references to the traditional **ballets** of Tchaikovsky and Prokofiev. But this is not a trivial, light-hearted **production**, the ugliness of rape and murder is clearly contrasted with the beautiful world of **fashion** and **advertising**. The use of a doppelganger to represent the deteriorating state of Dorian's conscience, rather than Wilde's magical **painting**, is skilful and touching.

Every stage in this **production** has been carefully thought out and there is a great increase of tension in the second half as the tragedy unfolds. The audience is left with the final image of the paparazzi rushing in to **photograph** Dorian's dead body, his lover already exploiting his fame and destruction as happened in real life with Princess Diana and Michael Jackson.

Audiences expect to find exciting and new **productions** at the Curve (Leicester's state of the art theatre, designed by the **architect** Rafael Vinoly) and they were not disappointed with this **production**. The sensation on entering this dramatically curved building was equalled by the sensuous and thought provoking **choreography** of Matthew Bourne.

Reflection 1.8

- How much does your own specialism or interest influence what you teach?
- What new genres or trends within the creative arts and media would you like to explore?

Business and the creative industries

The way in which the creative and media industries work as businesses is an important aspect for learners to understand. Many companies are small and medium enterprises (SMEs) with low numbers of people working in them. Many film production companies fit into this category. They will have a core staff and will buy in labour and expertise on a casual basis depending on the amount of work that they are involved in. Dance and theatre companies may work in the same way and musicians may belong to a number of orchestras in order to make a reasonable living from their music.

Learners need to understand that the creative and media industries are businesses that often rely on the symbiosis between creative arts and media areas. For example, a book may morph into a film, which can set a fashion trend, or a film may become a musical, then a television series, which spawns merchandising and websites. This has often been supported by vertical and horizontal integration. Frequently, there is news of mergers, where companies unite who are of equal importance or financial value and takeovers where a large company buys up a smaller company. Creative and media producers and owners need awareness and understanding of economics and how global businesses operate.

Vertical integration, in which a company takes over another company that operates at a different stage in the production line, has been a common business practice for years. A familiar example is the film studio that buys a chain of cinemas. Horizontal integration, in which a company buys another company carrying out the same type of work, has resulted in massive international creative and media companies. Learners who plan a career in the creative and media industries need to appreciate how the resulting globalization affects their employment prospects.

Reflection 1.9

How can you ensure learners gain understanding of the industry knowledge and research skills they will need when looking for a job in the creative and media industries and applying for work? The following task could be a starting point. Ask learners to find out about the owners of the following enterprises and other creative and media organizations they own or are subsidiaries. Ask them to reflect on why this information might be relevant.

- Channel Five
- New Ambassadors Theatre, London
- *Daily Telegraph*
- Your local radio station
- Tate St Ives
- Artavia advertising agency.

Sector skills councils

The sector skills councils (SSCs) aim to reduce skills gaps and shortages in the UK and increase productivity of the workforce in SMEs and large businesses. Through their work, they aim to keep the UK globally competitive. They conduct consultation work with industry, publish research and strategic documents, run projects and provide information about their industry sector. They identify the challenges facing industry and work on how to overcome these. They also take a lead role in working with education and employers to develop programmes of study.

Currently there are three sector skills councils for creative arts and media and it is interesting to note the areas that each one covers:

- Creative and Cultural Skills[7]
- Skillfast – UK[8]
- Skillset[9]

Creative and Cultural Skills

Creative and Cultural Skills (CCSkills) is the SSC for advertising, crafts, cultural heritage, design, literature, music, performing and visual arts. It recognizes that creative people need support in order to fulfil their potential. It also recognizes that creative businesses, especially micro businesses, need support to compete in international markets.

Creative and Cultural Skills research
CCSkills carried out the first study of the creative and cultural industries in 2006,[10] updating the data in 2008. The resulting statistics showed that:

- Total employment in the industry was 678,480.
- Design is the largest industry in employment terms in the creative and cultural industries.
- About 54 per cent of people working in the creative and cultural industries have at least a level 4 qualification and nearly a third have a level 2 or 3 qualification.
- Some 62 per cent working in the industries earn less than £20,000.
- While 59 per cent are employees, 41 per cent are self-employed.
- Self-employed workers (57 per cent) are more likely to have level 4 and above qualifications than employed workers (50 per cent).
- The visual arts has the highest proportion of people who are self-employed.
- Around 27 per cent of people in the creative and cultural industries work on a part-time basis.
- There is a majority of male workers.
- The number of women in the industry has grown by 13 per cent between 2006 and 2008, more than double the growth in male employment.
- Some 70 per cent of women in the industry earn less than £20,000 compared to 57 per cent of men.
- Most people (93 per cent) in the cultural industry are white; this varies little across the sector.
- About 54 per cent of the creative and cultural industries workforce are below the age of 40.
- There are 74,640 businesses in the creative and cultural industries, 87 per cent of them employing fewer than 10 people.
- Only 7 per cent of these businesses have a turnover of more than £1 million per year.

Skillfast – UK

Skillfast – UK is the SSC for fashion and textiles, a diverse and fast changing sector that needs to be responsive to the demands of a global marketplace. It covers materials production and processing, product design (textiles, clothing, fashion design), manufacture of made-up articles (such as footwear and leather goods), trading in, distribution and servicing (such as carpet fitting and dry-cleaning) of apparel, footwear and textile items.

Skillfast research
Information gathered by the sector[11] indicates that:

- Manufacturing, trading and servicing of fabric are dominated by small and medium-sized employers. More than 80 per cent of establishments have 10 employees or fewer.

- Although there are very few large employers (establishments with 200+ employees) these account for around one-fifth of the people employed in the sector.

- The apparel, footwear and textiles sector is split fairly evenly between men (48 per cent) and women (52 per cent) though this varies; different parts of the sector have different gender patterns (for example, men are more prevalent in the shoe repair trade, and women in clothing manufacturing).

- The sector is a major source of employment for people from ethnic minorities.

- The sector has an ageing workforce, with around 73 per cent aged 35 or over.

- Historically, employment in the sector has been concentrated in lower-skilled occupations, rather than in professional and administrative roles. However, the profile of the industry is changing, with manufacturing operations moving overseas, but management occupations remaining in the UK.

- Part-time employment in the sector is slightly below the UK economy average but certain parts of the sector (such as manufacturing, washing and dry-cleaning) have a very high level of part-time work.

- The sector has a high level of self-employment relative to the economy as a whole – particularly in the areas of washing, dry-cleaning and shoe repair.

Skillset

Skillset is the SSC for Creative Media, which comprises TV, film, radio, interactive media, animation, computer games, facilities, photo imaging and publishing. It provides extensive careers advice for both students and professionals, accredits courses and approves providers for these courses.

Skillset research

The Skillset Employment Census 2009 covers employment in television, radio, animation, facilities, interactive media, commercials, corporate production and all film sectors apart from production, photo imaging and performers.[12] Key facts from the resulting data include the following:

- Since the Census was carried out previously in 2006, there has been a major decline in every sector except independent production and cinema exhibition. The areas hit hardest are terrestrial broadcast, special physical effects, corporate production and computer games.

- Total employment in the sectors covered is estimated at 188,150 down from 202,000 in 2006. However, information on the employment sectors excluded by the Census (film production, photo imaging, performers, publishing and freelancers not working on Census Day) indicates that total creative media employment remains around 500,000 people.

- Overall, around a quarter of the workforce is freelance (24 per cent), a slight decrease from 27 per cent in 2006. Freelancing is most prevalent in those areas most closely involved in the production process.

- In 2006, 60 per cent of the industry worked in London and the South East. However, the relocation of part of the BBC's workforce from White City (in West London) to Salford Quays (near Manchester) in the North West increased employment in the North West from 6 per cent to 9 per cent and decreased employment in West London from 16 per cent to 13 per cent.

- Representation of women has fallen dramatically from 38 per cent in 2006 to 27 per cent and has fallen most sharply and is lowest in interactive media, games, commercials and corporate production, and has dropped least and remains highest in broadcast television, radio, and film production.

- Representation of black and ethnic minorities rose in 2006 to 7.4 per cent but has now dropped slightly to 6.7 per cent. The 2006 Census showed that the employment of ethnic minorities is above average in cable and satellite, processing laboratories and cinema exhibition but make up less than 5 per cent of the workforce in areas such as animation, computer games, radio broadcasting, offline multimedia and film distribution.

- Overall, the proportion of the workforce described by their employers as having a disability has remained the same since 2006, at 1.0 per cent. However, in Skillset's 2008 Creative Media Workforce Survey (which covered the same sectors as the Census apart from film production, which was accommodated separately), 5.8 per cent of the workforce said they had a disability.

Important information about creative arts and media industries can be found on the sector skills councils websites. On the Skillset website, for instance, there are sections for teachers including information on qualifications, careers news and information on Skillset's Academy Network.

Some parts of the creative arts and media industries at the margins are covered by other sector skills councils such as People First, the SSC for Hospitality and Catering, which covers visitor attractions and tourist services, and Skills Active, the active sport and leisure SSC that covers event management.

Reflection 1.10

- Study the information about employment above. What similarities and what differences are there in employment in the different sectors? Identify and prioritize the key factors that might affect progression into the industry for your learners. For example, they may live in the south west of England, or perhaps they are female learners who wish to enter the computer games industry?

- Consider how you can use the sector skills websites to support delivery. How can you encourage learners to use the careers information on these websites to motivate them and enable them to make realistic career choices?

There is a wealth of other regulatory, official or public bodies that can supply up-to-date information and advice. Most of their websites include links specifically for teachers. You might explore the websites of the following organizations and identify which sections would be useful for learners to access and which would be useful to support your own professional development.

- British Board of Film Classification (BBFC)
- British Broadcasting Corporation (BBC)
- National Theatre
- Arts Council England
- Advertising Standards Authority (ASA)
- National Union of Journalists (NUJ)
- Royal Academy
- Royal Academy of Dramatic Art (RADA)
- Equity

Reflection 1.11

- How do we promote equality and diversity in creative arts and media teaching and learning when the industry often expects its employees to segment audiences and produce products and performances that may be unethical, for example adverts that encourage overspending, films that show explicit violence, magazines that provide poor role models for women?
- How as teachers do we use all of the opportunities at our disposal to develop creative skills in our learners, when the creative and media products they consume relate more to instant celebrity than tenacity, hard work and originality of thought?

This chapter has explored the nature of creativity and the creative arts and media processes as well as the different industries in which they are used. We hope it has encouraged you to think about your own creativity and about the attributes and skills that your learners will need to be successful on their programme and in their future creative life.

References

1   Petty, G. (2006) *Evidence Based Teaching: A Practical Approach*. Cheltenham: Nelson Thornes.
2   Rowling, J.K. (2003) *Harry Potter and the Order of the Phoenix*. London: Bloomsbury.
3   Roger W. Sperry Site. Available from: www.rogersperry.info/ [Accessed 20 July 2010].
4   Centre for Educational Research and Innovation (CERI) and Organization for Economic Cooperation and Development (OECD) (2007) *Understanding the Brain: The Birth of a Learning Science*. Paris: OECD.
5   Jefferies, S. (2009) Inside the mind of an actor (literally). *Guardian* 24 November. Available from: www.guardian.co.uk/science/2009/nov/24/fiona-shaw-neuroscience [Accessed 8 April 2010].

6   de Bono, E. (1999) *Six Thinking Hats*. London: Penguin.
7   Creative and Cultural Skills. Available from: www.ccskills.org.uk [Accessed 20 July 2010].
8   Skillfast – UK. Available from: www.skillfast-uk.org/ [Accessed 20 July 2010].
9   Skillset. Available from: www.skillset.org/ [Accessed 20 July 2010].
10   CCSkills (2009) *The Creative and Cultural Skills 'Footprint': 08–09*.2009. Available from: www.ccskills.org.uk/Industrystrategies/Industryresearch/tabid/600/Default.aspx. [Accessed 8 April 2010].
11   Skillsfast. *Skillsfast Sector Overview*. Available from: www.skillfast-uk.org/about.cfm [Accessed 8 April 2010].
12   Skillset (2009) *Skillset Employment Census 2009*. Available from: www.skillset.org/uploads/pdf/asset_14487.pdf?5 [Accessed 11 October 2010].

Further reading

Adair, J. (2007) *The Art of Creative Thinking: How to be Innovative and Develop Great Ideas*. London: Kogan Page.
Bowkett, S. (2006) *100 Ideas for Teaching Creativity*. London: Continuum.
Claxton, G. and Lucas, B. (2007) *The Creative Thinking Plan: How to Generate Ideas and Solve Problems in your Work and Life*. Harlow: BBC Active.
Cowley, S. (2005) *Letting the Buggers be Creative*. London: Continuum.
de Bono, E. (1990) *Lateral Thinking: A Textbook of Creativity*. London: Penguin.
Gibbs, G. (1998) *Learning by Doing: A Guide to Teaching and Learning Methods*. London: Further Education Unit.
Robinson, K. (2001) *Out of Our Minds: Learning to be Creative*. Oxford: Capstone.

2

Creative arts and media programmes

By the end of this chapter, you will be able to:

- Explain the key features of programmes of learning that meet learners' aspirations and needs
- Understand the qualifications framework and the content, structure and mode of assessment for creative arts and media qualifications
- Recognize the key creative arts and media qualifications and their features

---

Introduction

Qualifications are always changing. Between our writing this book and your reading of it, a number of creative arts and media qualifications will have been introduced, revised or axed. However, many of the features of qualifications will remain the same and we hope that discussing these will guide you in choosing and delivering programmes of learning that are appropriate for your learners.

The tabloid press loves controversy about 'falling standards' and a lack of 'intellectual rigour' in qualifications that focus on a skills agenda. Such comments may be based upon the writers' own experiences and qualifications rather than an objective and detailed look at what a qualification requires learners to achieve and how the qualification is a response to changes in employment, technology, culture and society.

This chapter begins by looking at creative arts and media learners, their aspirations and needs, and how these can be matched with the key features of learning programmes. It is essential for funding purposes that learners follow an accredited programme and there is an in-depth exploration of the qualifications framework and how they indicate the level and content of the qualifications that sit within them. In the final section, existing and newer, vocational and academic creative arts and media qualifications are described so that you the teacher can compare and reflect on their suitability for your learners.

Learners' aspirations and needs

When you begin teaching, it is usual to be presented with a number of programmes on which you are expected to deliver; it is most likely that the first time you teach on these courses the learners will already have been enrolled, or following options sessions, inducted into the programme of study. All providers of education for the 14+ age group, including schools, consider the progression opportunities for their learners. Sometimes it is tempting for providers and individual teachers to recruit learners on to established programmes that attract large numbers and give good retention and achievement figures. This is less challenging than making the needs of individual learners the starting point or introducing new courses and qualifications that will support their progression into employment or further or higher education.

Even though learners may achieve good grades, it does not always mean that they will be able to progress. They may not have developed the appropriate skills for the next level course, such as the development of personal learning and thinking skills or technical skills such as using editing software. They may not have developed the English, mathematics or ICT skills needed to work in a particular job.

Qualifications are always changing and there may be other qualifications out there that better suit the needs of your learners. Before looking at different types of programmes and courses, we will consider what learners' aspirations might be.

Reflection 2.1

- How confident are you that your learners are always on the right programme for them?
- What is the process in your school, college or other learning organization that you go through to identify and introduce new programmes of study?
- When was the last time you investigated different qualifications from those you are delivering?

Who are our creative arts and media learners?

There are many different cohorts of creative arts and media learners in 14+ education. Apart from pupil, student or learner, they are often 'labelled' in some other way:

- Vocational learners
- Adult learners
- Learners in the 14–19 age group
- Unemployed learners
- Learners with learning difficulties and disabilities (LLD learners)
- Learners in secure estates
- Learners for whom English is a second or other language (ESOL learners)
- Full-time learners

- Part-time learners
- People not in employment, education or training (NEETs learners)

Reflection 2.2

- Do you think learners' creative arts and media aspirations and motivations are affected by being labelled as being in any of the above categories, for example retired people need watercolour classes, unemployed male teenagers need popular music workshops?
- What is the impact on learner choice of belonging to two or more of the above categories?

Learners' aspirations

Often learners themselves are unclear about their aspirations or why they are on a course. Questions as to why they want to study on a particular programme often elicit vague answers such as 'I like music', 'I am good at drawing' or 'I want to work in the media' or even 'My mates chose this and I like being with them'. An effective careers education and information, advice and guidance (CEIAG) and recruitment process should draw out of them what they hope to achieve by joining a learning programme and whether their aspirations and expectations of the programme are realistic.

However, learners can do this only if the information, advice and guidance they receive is comprehensive, objective and impartial and really does cover all of the options open to them as individual learners rather than as one of the categories suggested above.

Reflection 2.3

Table 2.1 is intended to help you to think about the reasons that learners have for enrolling onto creative arts and media programmes. Look at the headings in the table, which give reasons for coming on a programme. There may be others you wish to add to the list. Then look at the range of statements that learners might offer for why they want to join a programme of learning. You may want to add more of these, perhaps identified through a brainstorming activity with colleagues. Arrange these under the headings. You may find you identify other statements you have heard from learners as you go through the exercise. It is best if this activity is done with a colleague or colleagues who have the same set of learners so that you can compare results. You may want to cut up the headings and statements and put them on cards. It is always useful to save a few blank ones to add as you complete the exercise.

Think about the following:

- Which statements come under more than one heading (you will have to duplicate some cards)?
- Are some reasons considered more worthwhile than others? By you? Your colleagues? Your managers? By the learners themselves?

- Do any of these attract enhanced or additional funding for the organization or the programme? Does this make a difference?
- Which statements do you consider to be inappropriate or unacceptable to you?
- Which reasons would be valid for learners in a group that you teach?

Headings

The headings in Table 2.1 give reasons for coming on a programme.

Table 2.1 Reasons for joining a creative arts and media programme

For cultural purposes	For recreational purposes	To increase employability skills	To progress to higher education
To improve mental well-being	To improve social well-being	To improve physical well-being	For financial reasons
To gain a wider range of skills or enhanced skills	To increase knowledge of a subject area	*Add your own headings here*	*Add your own headings here*
Add your own headings here	*Add your own headings here*	*Add your own headings here*	*Add your own headings here*

Learners' statements

- I tried learning the piano when I was young but it didn't last so now I want to try again.
- Learning salsa helps me relax after a day at work.
- Learning about advertising will help the family business.
- My friend wants me to come with her to the art class for company.
- I am planning to go to drama college next year.
- My parents said I had to do a recognized qualification.
- I have arthritis in my hand so painting is a type of exercise.
- I had my daughter when I was 16. I'm a single parent and I get the Care to Learn payment. I need to do something with my life, for her sake.
- I like the drum tutor, she gave me lots of confidence.
- I want to be able to do voluntary work at the local hospital radio station.
- If I can pass my A level in media studies, I can get promotion at work.
- I want to set up a photography business.
- My partner likes to go to classical music concerts so I thought it would help me appreciate the music she likes.

- I did really well in media last year so now I want to specialize in computer gaming.
- The clarinet classes meant that I could join the local orchestra.
- Gain a dance qualification: it's important to me, it will give me self-esteem, it's something I can do.
- I want to learn how to play an instrument better. Perhaps I can join an orchestra and develop a social life.
- I want to get my short stories published by a magazine.
- I want to be prepared for a coach trip visiting art galleries in Italy this summer.
- I need a higher level qualification to do work at the local newspaper office.
- My employer gives me day release and pays for the course if I come to college to do the art course.

Key features of creative arts and media programmes of learning

Learners are faced with a wide range of creative arts and media courses and often are bewildered by the choice. Some providers tag their courses with information about what the course provides, what learners can expect to do on the course and other information regarding entry requirements and progression:

- Course title
- Attendance pattern
  - Part-time/full-time or block release etc.
- Course duration
- Entry requirements
- Details about the course delivery
  - How the course is taught
  - Who it is suitable for
  - Description of course content
  - How it is assessed
- Typical progression routes
- What you can expect from the organization
- What the organization expects from you
- Start time
- Start date
- Fee.

The key features that most learners are concerned about are listed below, together with clarification and examples. These are not in any particular order. Different learners will have different priorities.

Content of the programme

Learners need to know what content will be covered and whether the course is general (such as a media studies course) or specialist (a watercolour class).

Level of the programme

A programme may introduce new skills and knowledge or build on existing skills or knowledge. As the levels get higher, the skills and knowledge may increase in complexity and demands either a greater depth or breadth of experience or conversely increased specialism. A programme should offer reasonable challenge and help a learner progress. For many learners progression is going from one level to another, for example from a level 1 Foundation Creative and Media Diploma to the Higher Diploma and then the Advanced Diploma. The former Department for Children Schools and Families (DCSF) defined progression as 'an individual learner's progression from engagement in learning to further stages of learning and employment to fulfil personal, professional and/or academic aspirations'. However, it is essential that learners enrol on a programme that is appropriate for their ability and realistic aspirations (see the section below on initial assessment). Progression may also include gaining a wide range of skills at the same level. So a learner may want to take a grade 8 piano and a grade 8 violin qualification. (For more information on levels, see pp. 28–9 on the National Qualifications Framework and the Qualifications Credit Framework.)

Location of the programme

Learners need to know where their learning will take place, whether in a classroom, studio (e.g. a design, photographic, dance, recording, television studio) or in the workplace (e.g. a theatre) or a mixture of these. They are usually keen to know what technology they will have access to in the learning environment. The actual location of the college or work area may be a key consideration for some learners who may have mobility or transport issues. Consortia delivering the Diploma in Creative and Media will want to use the best resources that the consortium can offer and this may necessitate moving to different schools and colleges within the consortium.

Day and time when the programme runs

A major consideration for learners is whether a course is full-time or part-time and when classes will be held: the time of day and the day of the week. The time of courses can be critical for learners who may need to fit learning in with their job, access to public transport or childcare. Some learners may want a flexible learning programme that enables them to work from home and negotiate when they come into the educational establishment.

Length of the programme

Many full-time courses still start in September and may run for any length of time from an intensive two-week course in a specialist subject such as creative writing for radio to a two-year course in performing arts. Some programmes such as instrumental tuition may not have a definite end, but relate to the progress made. Learners need to understand what they are committing themselves to when joining a programme. Colleges can have flexibility as to when they may start a programme of study. Schools generally have little flexibility in this way.

Mode of assessment of the programme

Assessment may be through a summative examination or project, continuous assessment or a mixture of assessment processes. Some learners perform well in formal examinations and in some areas, such as musical performance, the experience of performing can prepare learners for the stress and requirement to perform to a consistently high standard in public concerts. Other learners prefer to demonstrate their knowledge and skills over a more extended timescale by carrying out a project or responding to an assignment brief. (For more information on assessment, see Chapter 7.) Most courses are certificated with learners aiming to achieve an accredited qualification (see pp. 29–30 on the National Database for Accredited Qualifications). However, even if learners are on a course that is not certificated by an awarding body, organizations have a requirement to provide feedback and formative assessment.

Proportion of theoretical work to practical work

Some learners prefer to develop their learning through academic programmes which are often knowledge based, that have an emphasis on theory and involve a high level of reading, research and writing. Other learners prefer more vocational programmes that have an emphasis on applied learning and practical skills.

Guided learning hours

The guided learning hours (GLH) indicate the length or size of the course and the depth of study expected. The Learning and Skills Council (LSC) defined GLH as 'all times when a member of staff is present to give specific guidance towards the learning aim being studied on a programme'. So for creative arts and media programmes, GLH can include lectures, tutorials, performance rehearsals, supervised studio work and the assessment of work where the learner is present as in an NVQ (see p. 37). It does not include hours where supervision is general and not specific to the study of learners, such as learners researching in a library for a design project. A level 3 full-time vocational course in media will have more GLH than a level 2 media course.

Structure of the programme

Larger programmes of learning such as a performing arts national diploma might consist of a series of units or modules, each of which is independently assessed, some or all of which may contribute to the achievement of the entire programme. These units or modules may be delivered consecutively or with blocks of two or three delivered at the same time.

Teaching team

Some programmes of study where, for example, learners learn to play a musical instrument will require individual or small group tuition. Many learners appreciate that an individual teacher or tutor will manage the whole of their learning experience. However, many larger programmes will involve a number of different teachers, some of whom may be specialists. Industry professionals may also be involved in delivering parts of the programme. The reputation and experience of the teaching team can be a key factor in attracting and retaining learners. In such a dynamic area as creative arts and media, it is extremely important for the teaching team to keep themselves up-to-date and for them to be aware of the changes in technology and practices to be able to support the development of their learners and to maintain their professional credibility.

Additional support

Additional support is usually defined as support for students with learning difficulties and disabilities (SLDD), but it can also include support from functional skills tutors, learning support workers, technicians, the careers guidance team and counsellors.

Approaches to delivery

Individual creative and media learners may have particular learning preferences, but all learners benefit from a range of pedagogic approaches and different types of activities from quizzes, debates and essay writing to enterprise challenges, electronic presentations, tests and project work.

Individual or group work

Some learners such as those on computer games or fine art courses may want a programme that allows them to work in a predominantly independent way while other learners, such as performing arts students or video production learners want the opportunity to work in teams. It is worth mentioning here that one of the most important skills that employers wish to see in their workforce is teamwork and learners prepare to face the challenges of the world of work, and particularly the creative and media industries, by developing as wide a range of employability and generic skills as possible.

Use of technology

There are still some learners such as those on a fine art, dance or acoustic instrumental tuition course who may have a limited use of technology as part of their course and may use computers only to word process written work or research. However, some learners such as those on music recording, design or theatrical lighting courses will use a high level of technology and software that approaches, or often matches industry standards.

Applied or work-based learning

Some programmes are delivered entirely in the workplace; others may involve extended work experience. All learners will benefit from some type of industry link that can range from a visit from an industry professional such as a newspaper editor to a master class run by a well-known jazz musician. Whatever the course or reason for learning, learners need to understand the professional requirements and be able to critically apply them to their work. (For more on applied learning, see Chapter 5.)

Homework or independent practice

Many creative arts and media programmes and particularly those in art and design and performing arts expect a high level of independent practice outside of the class. Musicians may well spend an hour each day practising their singing or instrumental playing. Longer creative arts and media programmes, such as an A level in film studies, will expect learners to write, carry out research and analyse films in their own time. 'Homework' for the sake of it can be demotivating. Learners need to see the work they do outside the more formal learning environment as engaging, relevant and as an opportunity to enhance their learning.

Cost of the programme

The financial cost of a creative arts and media programme can be the most significant factor as to whether a learner enrols on a course or not. Some learners may have to pay course fees for some programmes, particularly short courses. There may also be costs associated with travel or the purchase of items such as art materials, musical instruments, dance shoes or textbooks.

Progression after the programme

Many learners will want to know that the course will enable them to progress into employment, to further education or enhance their personal life.

Reflection 2.4

Describe, for a prospective learner, a creative arts and media programme on which you teach, using the headings above. Consider the following:

- How you will explain how the programme meets their expectations
- What will be the learning outcomes
- Your expectations of them
- The opportunities for progression.

Once you have identified the detail of all the elements within your programme, rank them to reflect your priorities. Think about:

> • How much does your order reflect the rank order of importance for most learners?
> • Which elements might affect learners' ability to attend a course regularly and complete their programme?

Qualifications frameworks and creative arts and media qualifications

Qualifications frameworks group together into levels, qualifications that place the same demands on learners with regard to knowledge, understanding and skills.[1] However, within a level, some qualifications may focus on one subject area such as dance while others include a mix of subjects (see the section on the Diploma in Creative and Media (pp. 35–6) for an example) and will take longer to complete. The frameworks show how a learner might progress within the education system and ensure that qualifications have a value and quality that can be recognized by learners and employers. Only qualifications that have been accredited by the three regulators for England, Wales and Northern Ireland can be included in the National Qualifications Framework (NQF).

The first three frameworks below cover qualifications recognized in England, Northern Ireland and Wales. The Scottish Credit and Qualifications Framework and Partnership provides access to all mainstream qualifications in Scotland.

- The NQF covers qualifications from entry level to level 8 (and will be closed for new registrations from January 2011).
- The Qualifications and Credit Framework (QCF) is the newer framework for vocational or work-related qualifications covering entry level to level 8. In Wales, the QCF forms part of the Credit and Qualifications Framework Wales (CQFW).
- The Framework for Higher Education Qualifications (broadly covers qualifications from levels 4 to 8 such as certificates of higher education, higher national diplomas, degrees, masters and doctorates).
- The Scottish Credit and Qualifications Framework (differs in structure from the QCF and covers qualifications from levels 1 to 12).

Qualifications and Credit Framework

Many of the vocational qualifications on the QCF are new, work-related qualifications. They are designed to give learners the skills that employers are looking for. However, other qualifications already on the NQF have been revised for the QCF.

The QCF recognizes achievement through the award of credit for units and qualifications. The credit value is a measure of the notional 'learning time' that the average learner will take to achieve the learning outcomes of a unit. So, some units may be worth one credit, others may be worth three credits. One credit is the equivalent of ten hours of notional learning. This includes not only guided learning hours (GLH) but also other relevant activities the learner undertakes such as independent study. For all awarding organizations (AOs) and for all levels (which indicate the difficulty of a qualification):

- An award will equal 1–12 credits
- A certificate will equal 13–36 credits
- A diploma will equal 37+ credits (not to be confused with the Diploma in Creative and Media, which is a composite qualification).

In the lead-up to 2011, existing qualifications will be moved onto the QCF and some will change their titles to indicate the size of learning.

A QCF qualification is made up of 'chunks' of learning (units) and some of these may form part of more than one qualification. Some units will be shared across awarding organizations who will develop units in collaboration. The required number of credits in a qualification is determined by rules of combination. These rules list which units are mandatory, which are optional and which can be used as part of other qualifications.

Progression for learners will be more flexible, as learning can be divided into smaller steps and credits can be transferred between qualifications. Learners can bank credits as they move through the levels. Some qualifications can contain units at different levels as long as 50 per cent of the credit is at the level of the qualification. For other qualifications, all units will be at the same level.

Learners will have a unique learning number (ULN) and a unique learning record (ULR), which will help avoid duplication of learning chunks. The ULN is a centrally generated ten-digit identifier that will enable all learners over the age of 14 in England, Northern Ireland and Wales to build a lifelong record of their learning achievements.

Foundation Learning Tier

Foundation Learning is the range of provision and learning for learners aged 14 to 19 who are predominantly working at entry level and level 1. It offers clear progression routes to a range of destinations at level 2. These routes or pathways might be to further programmes of learning, to employment (including supported employment), to independent living or to apprenticeships. All Foundation Learning programmes must include subject or vocational knowledge, skills and understanding, Functional Skills in English, mathematics and ICT (see Chapter 4) and personal and social development learning. Foundation Learning will allow a more personalized curriculum designed to raise learners' aspirations and engage them in lifelong learning.

National Database for Accredited Qualifications

The National Database for Accredited Qualifications includes information on all recognized awarding bodies and qualifications that are accredited by the government's regulatory organizations in England, the Office of Qualifications and Examinations Regulation (Ofqual); in Wales, Department of Children, Education, Lifelong Learning and Skills (DCELLS); in Northern Ireland, Council for the Curriculum, Examinations and Assessment (CCEA).[2]

At the time of writing, there are approximately 150 awarding bodies or awarding organizations listed on the database. Some of these are large organizations such as

City and Guilds or Edexcel. However, there are also smaller or more specialist organizations including the London Academy of Music and Dramatic Art (LAMDA), the British Ballet Organization, Rock School Ltd and the National Council for the Training of Journalists (NCTJ).

The database can be searched by:

- Sector (arts, media and publishing for creative arts and media qualifications)
- Subject (e.g. performing arts)
- Job role (e.g. dancer)
- Level (e.g. entry level, level 3)
- Type of qualification (e.g. AS level, diploma).

Further information on qualifications and specifications should be downloaded from individual awarding organizations' websites.

Reflection 2.5

Job roles are listed alphabetically on the National Database for Accredited Qualifications, e.g. under 'A' you will find:

- Actor/actress
- Advertising art director
- Animator
- Art administrator
- Art therapist
- Art valuer
- Audio-visual technician

You could ask your learners to search alphabetically for a job they aspire to and research the qualifications that might help them gain this job. Alternatively, you could split learners into pairs or small groups and ask them to research and compare qualifications for all creative and media job roles listed under a particular letter of the alphabet. The pairs or small groups would then feed back their findings to the whole group and could contribute to the compilation of a qualifications progression list for reference. It is interesting to note that a search under 'dancer' brings up over twice the number of qualifications than for performing arts. Why do you think that is?

Types of qualifications

This section describes different types of qualifications, with examples of their content and also case studies of why qualifications were selected to meet learners' needs. Table 2.2 (adapted from the DirectGov website)[3] describes the standard of learning expected at each level from entry level to level 6. You might also like to go on the National Database of Accredited Qualifications website and explore opportunities for levels 7–8 to which your learners might aspire.

Table 2.2 Creative arts and media qualifications on the National Qualifications Framework

NQF level	What qualifications at this level provide	Example of a creative arts and media qualification at this level
Entry level	• Basic knowledge and skills • Ability to apply learning in everyday situations • Not geared towards specific occupations	OCR Entry Level Certificate in Art and Design Ascentis Entry Level Certificate in Art EDEXCEL Entry Level BTEC Award in Performing Arts (Entry 3) WJEC Entry Level Certificate in Drama NOCN Entry Level Certificate in Media Literacy (Entry 3) WJEC Entry Level Certificate in Media Studies
Level 1	• Basic knowledge and skills • Ability to apply learning with guidance or supervision • May be linked to job competence	EDEXCEL Level 1 BTEC Diploma in Art and Design OCR Level 1 National Award In Applied Art and Design and Media AQA Applied GCSE in Media LAMDA Level 1 Award in Performance TVU Level 1 Graded Examination in Drama Trinity Guildhall Foundation Graded Examination in Drama CCEA Level 1 GCSE in Journalism in the Media and Communications Industry RSL Level 1 Foundation Diploma in Creative and Media
Level 2	• Good knowledge and understanding of a subject • Ability to perform variety of tasks with some guidance or supervision • Appropriate for many job roles	UAL Level 2 Certificate in Preparing to Work in Creative Media EDEXCEL Level 2 BTEC Certificate in Interactive Use of Media WJEC Applied Art and Design GCSE City and Guilds Level 2 Diploma in Creative Techniques in 2D City and Guilds Level 2 NVQ in Machine Printing AQA Level 2 GCSE in Expressive Arts Grades A*–C EDEXCEL Level 2 BTEC Certificate in Performing Arts

(Continued overleaf)

Table 2.2 Continued.

NQF level	What qualifications at this level provide	Example of a creative arts and media qualification at this level
		BBO Intermediate Vocational Graded Examination in Dance
		EDI Level 2 National Award In Music Business (Recording Industry)
		City and Guilds Level 2 Certificate in Photographic Make-up
		OCR Level 2 National Diploma in Media
		City and Guilds Level 2 NVQ in Grip for the Creative Industries
		City and Guilds Level 2 NVQ in Photo Imaging
		AQA Level 2 Higher Diploma in Creative and Media
Level 3	• Ability to gain or apply a range of knowledge, skills and understanding, at a detailed level • Appropriate if you plan to go to university, work independently, or (in some cases) supervise and train others in their field of work	OCR Level 3 AS GCE in Art and Design
		NCFE Level 3 Certificate in Creative Craft using Pattern Cutting
		CSkills Awards Level 3 NVQ in Set Crafts
		UAL Level 3 Certificate in Drawing (QCF)
		NCFE Level 3 Certificate in Creative Craft using Carnival Crafts (QCF)
		City and Guilds Level 3 Award in Creative Techniques in Interior Decor – Kitchen and Utility Room (QCF)
		City and Guilds Level 3 NVQ in Digital Print Production
		LAMDA Level 3 Graded Examination in Musical Theatre for the Actor/Singer
		EDI Level 3 National Award in Technical Theatre (Costume and Wardrobe)
		Cambridge International Level 3 Pre-U Certificate in Music
		EDEXCEL Level 3 BTEC Extended Diploma in Performing Arts (QCF)
		EDEXCEL BTEC Level 3 Certificate in Music Technology (QCF)

IBO Level 3 Certificate in HL Music

RSL Level 3 Diploma for Applied Music Practitioners

Trinity Guildhall Level 3 Graded Examination in Music Performance

ABC Level 3 Diploma in Sound Design and Music Technology

AQA Level 3 Advanced GCE in Media Studies

UAL Level 3 Diploma for Focus Pullers

City and Guilds Level 3 NVQ in Production for Television

NCTJ Level 3 Certificate in Journalism

City and Guilds Level 3 NVQ in Grip for the Creative Media Industries

EDI Level 3 National Award in Community Arts Management

AQA Progression Diploma in Creative and Media

EDEXCEL Advanced Diploma in Creative and Media

NCFE Level 3 Extended Certificate in Business for the Creative Industries

| Level 4 | • Specialist learning, involving detailed analysis of a high level of information and knowledge in an area of work or study
• Appropriate for people working in technical and professional jobs, and/or managing and developing others | EDI Level 4 Diploma in Conservation for the V&A

ABC Level 4 Diploma in Business for Creative Practitioners (QCF)

RSL Level 4 Certificate for Creative Practitioners

CIM Level 4 Professional Certificate in Marketing |
| Level 5 | • Ability to increase the depth of knowledge and understanding of an area of work or study, so you can respond to complex problems and situations
• Involves high level of work expertise and competence in managing and training others
• Appropriate for people working as higher grade technicians, professionals or managers | EDEXCEL Level 5 BTEC Higher National Diploma in Fine Arts

LAMDA Level 5 Diploma in Speech and Drama Education

EDEXCEL Level 5 BTEC Higher National Certificate in Fashion and Textiles

EDEXCEL Level 5 BTEC Higher National Diploma in Performing Arts |

(Continued overleaf)

Table 2.2 Continued.

NQF level	What qualifications at this level provide	Example of a creative arts and media qualification at this level
Level 6	• A specialist, high-level knowledge of an area of work or study, to enable you to use your own ideas and research in response to complex problems and situations • Appropriate for people working as knowledge-based professionals or in professional management positions	EDEXCEL Level 5 BTEC Higher National Diploma in Interactive Media MRS Level 5 Advanced Certificate in Market and Social Research Practice TCL Level 6 National Diploma in Professional Production Skills CIM Level 6 Professional Diploma in Marketing TCL Level 6 National Diploma in Professional Dance Trinity Guildhall Level 6 Licentiate Diploma in Performing (LTCL/ LGSMD) TCL Level 6 National Diploma in Professional Musical Theatre

Table 2.2 provides only a very few examples of the awarding bodies and types of qualifications available at each level. In the table are listed some examples of GCSEs, AS, A levels and degrees that are part of traditional academic qualifications. However, an increasing number of qualifications are vocational or work-related qualifications that focus on learning practical skills. These include NVQs, City and Guilds, BTECs (awarded by the Business and Technology Education Council), OCR Nationals (awarded by Oxford, Cambridge and RSA Examinations) as well as the newer qualifications on the QCF. The table does not include Higher National Diplomas (HNDs) or degrees. However, the examples should give you a flavour of the variety of creative arts and media accredited qualifications that are out there and encourage you and your learners to explore what is available.

Key creative arts and media qualifications

Some of the qualifications listed below are well established, others are more recent. As you read this section, you might like to think about what makes these valuable to your learners, to employers and to parents or carers.

GCSEs

The General Certificate of Secondary Education (GCSE) was designed to encourage 16 year olds to study and enter for national qualifications at the age of 16. The qualification is currently the principal school-leaving qualification in England. Since 1988 when the first GCSEs were awarded, the content of individual qualifications has been updated to reflect innovations in teaching and learning and assessment arrangements have been revised to stretch and challenge candidates. GCSEs are often used as an entry requirement for level 3 study.

In 2001, the government decided to introduce new GCSEs in vocational subjects to give a vocational option to all young people and to promote vocational learning. The new GCSEs are available in twelve applied subjects and are double awards (that is twice the size and value of an academic GCSE). Applied Art and Design could be a qualification that schools and colleges may offer within the creative arts and media curriculum.

Short course GCSEs are designed to give learners more options about what and how they study. They are equivalent to half a full GCSE, so can be taken in half the time, usually over three terms, but could be taken over the same length as a traditional GCSE. Short course GCSEs allow more able students to take extra subjects, or can also be an option if timetable constraints prevent taking a full GCSE. Short course GCSEs are available in a range of traditional GCSE subjects and they lead to the same grades: A*–G and U. Progression from short course GCSEs may be limited if the requirements of level 3 qualifications, such as A levels, require a full GCSE in that subject.

The International General Certificate of Secondary Education (IGCSE or iGCSE) is an internationally recognized qualification for learners aged 14–16. It includes a range of subjects including the creative subjects.

A levels and AS levels

GCE Advanced levels (A levels) are the qualifications that the majority of young people use to gain entry to university. They consist of Advanced Subsidiary (AS) and A2 units. Each year over 780,000 A levels and 1 million AS levels are awarded. A levels are available in more than 80 subjects. There is a good range of creative arts and media subjects.

Diploma in Creative and Media

Diplomas are available in a range of subjects called 'lines of learning'. They are qualifications for 14–19 year olds, combining theoretical and practical learning.[4] Each diploma is a composite qualification. It consists of:

- Principal learning – these are the units in which learners develop skills that can be used in creative and media contexts (e.g. the theatre, the art workshop). They are required to develop a wide range of skills but the specifications suggest rather than dictate which specific creative and media skills should be delivered.
- Generic learning – these are functional skills in English, maths and ICT, personal, learning and thinking skills (PLTS). For more information on these, see Chapter 3.
- A standalone project (see below under 'Project').
- At least ten days' work experience.

- Additional or specialist learning are other qualifications which may broaden the learning experience to provide additionality (e.g. an A level in a language) or deepen the learning experience by a specialist qualification (e.g. a grade 8 guitar examination).

Each diploma is available at three levels: the foundation diploma is a level 1 qualification, the higher diploma is a level 2 qualification, and the advanced and progression diplomas are level 3 qualifications.

Project

The development of skills is a significant element of 14–19 reform. Learners working on well-planned, relevant and appropriate projects help to develop a wide range of skills that support progression beyond 14–19. The project is a mandatory component of the Diploma in Creative and Media and is an optional additional qualification for learners following GCSE, A level or other programmes at levels 1, 2 or 3.

BTEC and other national awards, certificates and diplomas

These are vocational qualifications that offer a learning programme that provides a practical approach to gaining industry knowledge and skills in a specific area such as performing arts, music technology, media, fashion or art and design. Assessment may be continuous and focuses on project work, skills audits and the collection of a portfolio of evidence.

Arts Award

The Arts Award 'aspires to support any young person to enjoy the arts and develop creative leadership skills'.[5] It is offered at levels 1 (bronze), 2 (silver) and 3 (gold) on the National Qualifications Framework.

Learners can complete an Arts Award in a single area or across a number of areas in the arts (e.g. fashion, creative writing, contemporary music, sculpture, film). Learners can create or perform their own work, or develop their skills in essential roles like marketing or stage management. They are required to set themselves an 'arts challenge', go to live events, research careers, share their skills with others, organize their project and put together a portfolio of work.

A key feature here is flexibility. The awards are designed to fit around learners' other commitments, and can be based in youth clubs, arts centres, schools, colleges, theatres or community groups.

Baccalaureate

On the International Baccalaureate Diploma Programme,[6] learners study six courses at higher level or standard level. Subject areas are divided into six groupings. Learners choose one subject from groups one to five to ensure breadth of experience. Learners typically study languages, social studies, the experimental sciences and mathematics.

The sixth subject may be an arts subject chosen from group six or may be another subject from groups one to five.

In addition, the programme has three core requirements that are included to broaden the educational experience and challenge students to apply their knowledge and understanding:

- The extended essay is a requirement for learners to engage in independent research through an in-depth study of a question relating to one of the subjects they are studying.
- 'Theory of knowledge' is a course designed to encourage each learner to reflect on the nature of knowledge by critically examining different ways of knowing (perception, emotion, language and reason) and different kinds of knowledge (scientific, artistic, mathematical and historical).
- 'Creativity, action, service' requires that learners actively learn from the experience of doing real tasks beyond the classroom. Learners can combine all three components or do activities related to each one of them separately.

NVQs

National Vocational Qualifications (NVQs) are qualifications delivered in the workplace or other settings that replicate the working environment.[7] These qualifications are outcome based with no prescribed learning programme, allowing for flexible delivery, and are tailored to meet the individual learner's needs.

NVQs are based on national occupational standards. These standards refer to outcomes that can be assessed and that define the competencies, knowledge and understanding needed in a given occupation. National occupational standards covering almost every occupation are presented as units and form the basis of all NVQs.

National occupational standards are set and designed by the relevant sector body. In the case of creative arts and media qualifications this is complicated by the way creative and media occupational areas are organized by UK Standards. Under the general heading of Arts, Media and Publishing, the following areas are identified: performing arts, crafts, creative arts and design, media and communication, and publishing and information services. There is considerable detail in the standards as they deal with practical skills such as changing the appearance of a performer through hair and makeup and detailing the requirements relating to health, safety and hygiene in carrying out this task. Most 14–19 teachers would not use the standards directly within their teaching, but they are useful to refer to when designing assignments or schemes of work. They could also be used as checklists for learners to enable them to relate their work to the industry as the standards spell out in considerable detail the expectations that workers within the industry need to be able to fulfil.

Apprenticeships

Opportunities for apprenticeships are increasing.[8] Creative apprenticeships allowing people to work in the industries, be paid and learn skills as they work, will be established in a range of creative and media areas such as live events and promotion, music business, technical theatre, costume and wardrobe, cultural venue operations and community arts. The advantage for employers is that they will have workers trained in relevant and appropriate skills.

Reflection 2.6

- How can you enable parents, carers, higher education institutions and employers to recognize the value of creative arts and media qualifications?
- What support and resources, including time, do you need to introduce new creative arts and media qualifications?
- To what extent do some qualifications reinforce the academic or vocational divide?

In this chapter, we have given you, to the best of our knowledge, a picture of the qualifications available to learners within the 14–19 age group. We have tried to contextualize creative arts and media programmes of learning within the bigger picture for two reasons. The first is that the creative arts and media curriculum does not exist in a vacuum. Often subjects in our area are studied alongside other subjects as in GCSE or A levels. The second reason is that the 14–19 curriculum is a complex picture and we hope that we have supported you in reflecting on how qualifications are selected to best serve the needs and aspirations of your learners. We hope you will continue with discussion about the issues, challenges and creative opportunities that exist for you in preparing to deliver your programmes.

References

1   Ofqual. Available from: www.ofqual.gov.uk/qualification-and-assessment-framework/89-articles/147-equivalent-qualifications [Accessed 22 July 2010].
2   National Database of Accredited Qualifications©. Available from: www.accreditedqualifications.org.uk/index.aspx [Accessed 22 July 2010].
3   Directgov. Available from: www.direct.gov.uk/en/EducationAndLearning/Qualifications Explained/DG_10039017 [Accessed 22 July 2010].
4   Directgov. Available from: www.direct.gov.uk/en/EducationAndLearning/Qualifications Explained/DG_070676 [Accessed 22 July 2010].
5   Arts Award. Available from: www.artsaward.org.uk/site/?id=64 [Accessed 23 July 2010].
6   International Baccalaureate Organization. Available from: www.ibo.org/diploma/ [Accessed 22 July 2010].
7   Directgov. Available from: www.direct.gov.uk/en/EducationAndLearning/Qualifications Explained/DG_10039029 [Accessed 22 July 2010].
8   notgoingtouni.co.uk. Available from: www.notgoingtouni.co.uk/advice/apprenticeships-available/creative-apprenticeships/ [Accessed 24 July 2010].

Useful websites

Information on curriculum and assessment in Northern Ireland: www.ccea.org.uk/ [Accessed 22 July 2010].

Information on curriculum and assessment in Scotland: www.sqa.org.uk/sqa/CCC_FirstPage. jsp [Accessed 22 July 2010].

Information on curriculum and assessment in Wales: http://new.wales.gov.uk/topics/ educationandskills/?lang=en [Accessed 22 July 2010].

Apprenticeships Case study: www.visionandmedia.co.uk/page/media-apprenticeships [Accessed 22 July 2010].

Further reading

Armitage, A., Bryant, R., Dunnill, R., Flanagan, K., Hayes, D., Hudson, A., Kent, J., Lawes, S., and Renwick, M. (2007) *Teaching and Training in Post-Compulsory Education*, 3rd edn. Maidenhead: Open University Press (Chapters 7 and 8).

Bloomer, M. (1997) *Curriculum Making in Post 16 Education*. London: Routledge.

Donovan, G. (2005) *Teaching 14–19: Everything You Need to Know about Teaching and Learning across the Phases*. London: David Fulton.

Harkin, J., Turner, G. and Dawn, T. (2001) *Teaching Young Adults*. London: Routledge.

Kelly, A.V. (1999) *The Curriculum, Theory and Practice*, 4th edn. London: Paul Chapman.

Wallace, S. (2001) *Teaching and Supporting Learning in Further Education*. London: Learning Matters.

3

Employability and life skills

By the end of this chapter, you will be able to:

- Understand why business and enterprise skills are needed by creative arts and media learners
- Embed the explicit learning of wider key skills and personal, learning and thinking skills (PLTs) into a creative arts and media programme of learning
- Recognize how functional skills can support learner progress

Introduction

Learners need a range of skills that will enable them to function in employment in the creative and media industries, as effective citizens and as lifelong learners. Learners need to recognize the usefulness of such skills so that they are motivated to practise them and have the confidence to use them in different contexts.

Chapter 1 dealt with the interrelationship between different creative arts and media disciplines and other sectors. In this chapter, a wide range of skills are explored in detail. These include:

- Employability, business and enterprise skills
- Wider key skills/personal, learning and thinking skills
- Skills for Life/functional skills in English, mathematics and ICT.

Higher functioning skills, which include ideas generation, research, and project management, are extremely important in the creative world and lie at the heart of creative and media teaching and learning. They are dealt with in Chapter 4.

Business and enterprise skills: skills and attributes for a changing world

The days when a person remained in the same employment for most of their working life have long gone. In the future most people will expect to change their jobs and the sector they work in several times.

Look at column 1 in Table 3.1. These are the roles carried out at different times by one of the authors. They overlap rather than occur consecutively. The second and third columns in Table 3.1 indicate the variety of skills and attributes needed to effectively carry out these roles. Many of these skills and attributes are transferable and overlap into a range of roles, for instance financial capability relates to working as a freelance musician and creative skills when working as a writer.

Such transferable and generic skills are in contrast with specialist skills that are useful only in limited contexts or may be associated with specific equipment or working practices. However, the development of transferable skills and specialist skills is closely entwined.

The temptation for a creative arts and media teacher at the beginning of a course is to start with delivery of specialist learning and neglect the explicit teaching and learning of generic and transferable skills that will motivate learners and enable them to produce work of a high standard effectively.

Table 3.1 Creative arts and media roles, transferable skills and attributes

Role	Transferable skills	Attributes
Librarian (music, art and local history)	Research skills Customer care skills Listening skills	Tidy Curious
Parent and home maker	Parenting skills Organizational skills Financial capability	Communicative Caring
Freelance musician (funeral organist, theatre pit violinist, accompanist, band member)	Entrepreneurial skills Effective participation skills Numeracy skills	Punctual Change loving
Self-employed piano teacher	Business skills Self-management skills	Enthusiastic Friendly
Teacher in FE	Creative skills Communication skills	Adaptability
Chief examiner or moderator	Team-building skills Reflective skills Decision-making skills	Logical Fair
Voluntary aid worker	Planning skills Problem-solving skills	Patient Open-minded
Writer (textbooks, Internet materials)	Enquiry skills English skills ICT skills	Hardworking Self-motivated

Leitch Report

The Leitch Report, which was published in December 2006, provided a compelling vision for the UK to be a leader in world-class skills by 2020.[1] It recognized that the UK still had a skills gap leaving it lagging behind other international economies. In his review, Lord Sandy Leitch painted a picture of exponential growth in production and in the skilling of the workforce in such emerging economies as India and China. To respond to this challenge from overseas, the report suggested that the UK needs to double attainment at all skill levels. Many of the skills that the creative arts and media disciplines help learners to develop are the skills of innovation, creativity and the development of an entrepreneurial approach that are essential to continue to drive the UK economy, not only within the creative industries but also across the economy as a whole.

The report put employability skills at the heart of the education and training agenda. It recognized the importance of a skilled workforce in helping employers achieve higher productivity and in keeping their businesses competitive. It also recognized the importance of improved skill levels essential for gaining better jobs and a higher income.

Leitch identified that for the UK economy to prosper, employees needed not only vocational skills and qualifications but also transferable skills such as literacy, numeracy, team working and communication skills. Targets were set so that by 2020 in England:

- Most adults (95 per cent) will have the basic skills of functional literacy and numeracy, up from 85 per cent literacy and 79 per cent numeracy in 2005 (basic being defined as level 1 literacy equivalent to a GCSE at grade D–G and entry level 3 numeracy).
- More than 90 per cent of adults will be qualified to at least level 2 (equivalent to five GCSEs at A*–C grades).
- The number of apprenticeships will be increased to 500,000 a year.
- More people (1.9 million) will attain level 3 (equivalent to two A levels).
- More than 40 per cent of adults will be qualified to level 4 and above.

You may also at this point wish to refer back to the sector skills councils' employment related research in Chapter 1 and consider the implications for learners. Creative and media industries have a high level of freelance workers. Self-employed people need to be multiskilled and able to handle all aspects of their business including production, financial management, marketing and sales.

Employability, business and enterprise skills

To be prepared for employment, whether paid or voluntary, learners need to develop not only appropriate skills but also appropriate personal attributes or qualities. They must develop skills and attributes that will enable them not only to gain employment but also to stay in employment and progress in a career.

The Institute of Directors' (IoD) research in 2007 identified which skills and qualities were particularly valued in graduate employees by company directors and how prevalent these skills were in new recruits.[2] The survey defined employability skills as 'the skills, attributes and abilities – other than technical competence – that make an employee an asset to their employer'. The survey showed that:

- About 40 per cent of IoD members thought that both graduates and non-graduates were unprepared for employment.
- Some 90 per cent of IoD members believed that the education system should do more to prepare young people for the world of work.
- Around 89 per cent believed that businesses should play a greater role in developing young people's employability skills.
- Foreign language skills, leadership skills and business acumen were among the employability skills graduate employers witnessed least frequently.
- Of the ten employability skills rated most important for graduates to possess (see below), the ability to meet deadlines was the one least likely to be demonstrated by new recruits.

The top ten skills and qualities rated as being most important for recent graduates were:

1 Honesty and integrity
2 Basic literacy skills
3 Basic oral communication skills (e.g. telephone skills)
4 Reliability
5 Being hardworking and having a good work ethic
6 Numeracy skills
7 A positive 'can do' attitude
8 Punctuality
9 The ability to meet deadlines
10 Team working and cooperation skills.

The skills and attributes mentioned above are generic; they are used in all industry sectors including the creative and media industries. Some of them will be dealt with in more detail in the following sections.

Reflection 3.1

- What level of knowledge do your learners have of local, regional, national and international job markets?
- Do they realize they will most likely be looking for employment in the creative and media industries in competition with learners from other countries and at some stage work freelance or have their own company?

Business skills

Learners with business and enterprise skills are increasingly seen as being attractive to employers. The development of these skills is particularly important for learners studying for qualifications such as the Diploma in Creative and Media, which has a focus on work experience, industry working practices and project working. There are a number of key business skills, discussed in the following subsections.

Business planning

Business planning includes preparing a business plan and assessing the strengths, weaknesses, opportunities and threats (SWOTs) for the business. An individual free-lance worker needs a business plan as much as a large company and is essential for anyone thinking of asking banks or other investors for loans.

The business plan will:

- Describe their creative arts and media venture whether it is a service or a product
- Identify the marketing and sales opportunities
- Suggest business strategies
- Recognize the current financial situation
- Include a financial forecast.

Financial management

Financial management covers cash flow planning, credit management, understanding bank and accountancy services. Many creative and media workers are freelance or work in small and medium enterprises (SMEs). Effective financial management skills (often referred as financial capability) are vitally important in order to finance every-day living and develop opportunities for further work. Project briefs may not involve creating a budget, but they will almost certainly have to work to a budget and under-stand the budgeting process. At start up, businesses can survive for a short while with low sales or profits but cash is essential. If a dancer or photographer does not under-stand cash flow management, they may find they do not have money to pay for travel to the next audition or photo shoot. Earnings made from a theatrical run or from a photographic exhibition may have to support them for several months when they are not working. Understanding banking and credit services can be vitally important. Whether they employ an accountant or not, creative arts and media workers need to be aware of what taxes they need to pay and when.

Product or service development

Product or service development includes resources (people, materials and processes) management, working with clients and customer care. Creative and media products and services that include fashion, entertainment and information require continuous development. The rate of technological change involved in production requires people who are adaptable and open to learning new skills and using new equipment, software and materials. The purpose of most creative and media businesses is to make a profit and this means that companies must work successfully with clients and customers who may be audiences, viewers, listeners, games players or readers. Customer care is not just the responsibility of the marketing team or company director. All employees are responsible for maintaining the image of the organization for which they work.

People management

People management involves recruitment, team building, motivating staff, resolving disputes, and providing training. Film and theatre directors and newspaper editors not only have to be personally creative but also need skills of people management. Motivating colleagues is not just the responsibility of a manager; it involves everyone in the production and other work processes. Being creative often involves bouncing ideas off others and working together to make a media product or theatrical performance work, so team working skills are essential. This is dealt with in more detail below in personal, learning and thinking skills.

Marketing

Marketing includes preparing a marketing plan and marketing reports, identifying the selling points of products or services, carrying out research, providing data and information on the marketplace, and creating advertisements and promotions. Even if their job is not primarily a marketing role, all workers should know about the marketplace in which they operate.

- What are the current trends?
- Who are the main competitors?
- How are consumers or audiences changing?

Creative arts and media learners trying to gain entry to the sector will have an advantage if they can show a prospective client or employer that they are aware of the marketplace for their ideas and skills and understand the marketing mix: product, price, place, promotion (4 Ps) and service. Freelance workers must of course be prepared to market themselves. The AIDA principle (Attract, Interest, arouse Desire and create Action) for advertising products could apply equally to someone attending an audition or interview!

Sales and distribution

Sales and distribution involve running sales operations and working with suppliers and customers or audiences. Sales and distributions operations will impact on the work of creative and media workers, even if working freelance for a company.

Their work will need to fit in with the overall schedule. For example, the publication date of this book was April 2011 so the authors had to complete their work by July 2010.

Operating legally and ethically

It is essential not only to have legal and ethical knowledge but also to know how to apply them. Media learners can often write about regulatory bodies such as the Advertising Standard Authority (ASA), Office of Communications (Ofcom) and British Board of Film Classification (BBFC) and describe the legislation or regulations associated with them but often, they do not check their own work to see if it is targeted at and appropriate for specific audiences or consumers.

Enterprise skills

Business and enterprise are terms that are often linked together and there are obviously some similarities in the skills and personal qualities needed for both setting up an enterprise and running a business.[3] Enterprise is defined in the Oxford dictionary as an 'undertaking, esp. bold or difficult one; readiness to engage in such undertakings' whereas the definition of business includes the following: 'task, habitual occupation, structure, commercial house, firm'.

Many of the attributes needed for setting up an enterprise are the same as those associated with creativity: bursting with new ideas, capable of original thought, able to have a fresh take on an existing product or service, daring to be different, wanting to be world changing, lateral thinking, inventive, resourceful, inspired, risk taking, single minded.

Reflection 3.2

Respond to the questions below by rating yourself on a scale 1–5 (with 1 being 'needs improvement' and 5 being 'I'm great at this'). If learners carry out this activity, they can compare their rating as entrepreneurs with their peers.

- Do you like to take the initiative?
- Do you embrace change?
- Do you want to make a difference in life or work?
- Can you imagine how the creative world might be in ten years' time?
- Can you make decisions?
- Do you like taking risks?
- Can you promote yourself or your organization?
- Are you financially capable?
- Can you organize resources?
- Can you meet challenges and overcome barriers?

Types of enterprise

Types of enterprise include the following:

- *Commercial enterprise* is where the main purpose of the enterprise is to make money. This might be as for example a sole trader supplying theatrical props or a limited company producing local radio advertisements.
- *Social enterprise* is a venture that benefits the wider community. An example of this is outreach activities in a large theatre where performances are taken into the community, to shopping centres or youth clubs.
- *Personal enterprise* improves the quality of an individual's life and work either for their own benefit or that of an organization in which they work. Examples of this include learning to play a musical instrument for one's own enjoyment or learning about art history to appreciate works of art in an art gallery. Within a media company an employee might show initiative in cutting travel costs or an employee in a dance company might come up with an idea for a new promotion for a theatre event.

Ideas generation lies at the heart of enterprise and is dealt with in more detail in Chapter 4.

Reflection 3.3

- When do learners have the opportunities to be enterprising within creative arts and media sessions?
- What holds you and your learners back from engaging with business and enterprise?
- Who might support you in delivering business and enterprise skills to learners, for example, banks and business organizations, Connexions, employers or creative partnerships? You can find out more about this type of support in Chapter 6.

Embedding the explicit learning of wider key skills and PLTS into a creative arts and media programme of learning

It has long been recognized that for learners to fulfil their potential both in and outside of the classroom, they need to develop generic skills that enable them to become successful learners and participators. The skills needed for this were called wider key skills and were grouped under the following headings:

- Improving own learning and performance
- Problem solving
- Working with others.

The 14–19 diplomas also recognize that learners need to develop a range of skills that prepare them for working effectively in different environments either as employees in industry or as individuals pursuing their own creative dreams.

Personal, learning and thinking skills

Personal, learning and thinking skills have been grouped together under six headings. Each group is distinctive, but there are links between them. They can be seen as a development of the wider key skills mentioned above.

Independent enquirers

Independent enquiry is a major skill area for professional creative and media practitioners. For example, a journalist has not only to collect information but also to evaluate it and consider the effect on other people of what is said or written. Creative arts and media learners are often curious, explorative people but the challenge can be to get them to use the research or information they collect in order to influence their products or performances. Teenagers in particular can be egocentric and can ignore the values and needs of their audiences or consumers of their creative and media products. This is discussed further in Chapter 4 on carrying out research.

Creative thinkers

The creative and media industries are dependent on a regular flow of new ideas. The UK economy requires creative thinking and ideas to create commercial success and innovation in all areas including engineering and medicine as well as in entertainment and information areas. Further discussion about creativity and the generation on ideas is in Chapters 1 and 4.

Reflective learners (wider key skills: improving own learning and performance)

Production and performance teams and particularly the thousands of freelance workers who operate in the creative and media sector need to be able to set targets and monitor their own performance and feedback. Learners can often find it difficult to be reflective, because although we all learn every day, we are not often aware of what we are learning and how we learn. This learning may include items of knowledge, an increased understanding of a process or situation, taking responsibility for their own learning by managing the way in which they learn, knowing how to set, review and improve targets, prioritize learning and locate and use support. By becoming 'expert' learners, the locus of the relationship with the teacher changes and is more likely to become one of partnership.

Team workers (wider key skills: working with others)

Nearly all creative arts and media people work in teams, which demands different skills and personal qualities than when an individual works on their own. If learners enjoy working in groups, this does not always mean that they understand how teams operate. Some creative arts and media learners can try to avoid working with others for a number of reasons: they may feel that others in the group will pull down their grades, they may not like some of the people they work with, they may have a different vision of what a final product or performance should be. This inability to work with others can hold up project work if not addressed at the beginning of a course. Learners may also not consider the teaching staff to be people with whom they have to work alongside. This skill enables learners to discuss and negotiate with others, clarify roles and responsibilities, decide on feasible timescales, give and receive support, agree on what and how to improve work and handle difficult situations and relationships. (For more information on team building, see pp. 75–7.)

Self-managers

A feature of much creative arts and media teaching is the move from 'front-of-class' delivery by one or two teachers to the teacher as facilitator, working in partnership with learners, teachers from other areas and with industry professionals. However, the teacher as facilitator requires learners to be more self-directive and take control over their own learning. The greatest challenge here can be for learners moving from an environment where teaching is more traditional and learning has been largely knowledge based.

Effective participators

Learners can be very active on their programme, handing in assignments on time, working well with others, being attentive in class but ignoring the need to participate with larger issues that they might encounter in life and work in the future. Effective creative arts and media learners who can generate new ideas and produce a high standard of work are often those who engage with the world outside the classroom. These are the learners who might belong to a local drama company, do voluntary work for a charity, join an environmental pressure or create a blog on an Internet.

Problem solving (wider key skills)

All creative work can be seen as problem solving. The problem for a sculptor may be to translate a transient feeling into a tangible form that can be interpreted by the viewer. The problem for a dance company may be to attract an audience or work to a tight budget. The problem for a games designer may be to work within ethical constraints regarding violence. Some problems encountered can be quick and easy to solve, for example, how to travel to a photo shoot. Other problems may take longer and more effort to solve, such as how to gain financial support for a new film project. This wider key skill helps learners to identify the nature of different problems, analyse problems, suggest and test different solutions and review solutions.

As you read about each set of skills, you will have realized that creative arts and media learners will be carrying out many learning activities that include these skills. An assignment that involves making a film, putting on a fashion show or staging a drama can 'tick all the boxes'. However, PLTS and wider key skills need to be taught explicitly and learners need multiple opportunities and formative assessment opportunities to develop these skills.

Delivering PLTS and wider key skills effectively

There are a number of ways in which PLTS and wider key skills can be delivered effectively. Here are some ideas:

- Introduce different sets of skills each week during an extended induction or tutorial period involving industry practitioners and case studies as well as hands on activities to engage learners and make the skills relevant for them.
- Before starting a major assignment, identify the level of PLTS or wider key skills. Build in activities that will support learners in working independently and plan sessions that include delivery of these skills.
- Work with colleagues across disciplines or subjects to create a PLTS-based curriculum.
- Issue learners with PLTS 'passports' or diaries so that they can record and self-assess when and how they have practised their PLTS. Encourage them to suggest activities and tasks they have carried out that demonstrate effective use of their PLTS.
- Identify small activities that focus overtly on one or two skills rather than wait until a major assignment or activity is carried out which will make observation, assessment and feedback of PLTS more complex and less immediate.

Look at Table 3.2. The left-hand column gives the learning outcomes for one group of PLTS (independent enquirers). The right-hand column gives an example of a simple, short activity or task that would support learners in achieving these outcomes. These might be used at the start of sessions as an icebreaker or as a homework task. Most are suitable as a small group or individual task or activity. These tasks have a creative and media flavour but introducing activities or tasks relating to other sectors is also a good idea to reinforce the concept that these are transferable skills.

Recognizing how functional skills can support learner progress

The Functional Skills Standards state that: 'Functional skills in English, mathematics and information and communication technology (ICT) help people to gain the most out of life, learning and work.'[4]

The skills are learning tools that enable people to do the following:

- Apply their knowledge and understanding to everyday life
- Engage competently and confidently with others
- Solve problems in both familiar and unfamiliar situations
- Develop personally and professionally as positive citizens who can actively contribute to society.

Table 3.2 Examples of creative arts and media activities to develop personal, learning and thinking skills

Learning outcomes	Examples of tasks or activities that might develop these skills
Independent enquirers Young people:	
• Identify questions to answer and problems to resolve	Learners prepare four key (interesting) questions for an interview with a celebrity or an industry specialist Learners brainstorm and prioritize problems that might prevent them going on an industry visit or a night out to the theatre or cinema. They should consider both the likely and the unusual problems
• Plan and carry out research, appreciating the consequences of decisions	Learners plan their time by identifying as many tasks as possible and create a Gantt chart that shows them how tasks overlap and how they fit into a timeline[5] Learners research the general public's favourite colour and use the results to influence the design of a costume, advertisement, magazine cover or log
• Explore issues, events or problems from different perspectives	Allocate four main characters from a soap or TV drama where the characters are familiar to learners. Give the learners five minutes to either role-play or describe their character's likely response to an event such as flooding or an issue such as drugs. The rest of the class observe and feed back their opinions
• Analyse and evaluate information, judging its relevance and value	Choose a 'hot' topic such as the design of a new car or a new celebrity fashion. Give learners different types of information about the topic from different sources e.g. news short from a tabloid, an in-depth article from a magazine, a TV advertisement, a quote from a parent, a quote from a teenager. Ask learners to give a star rating for each source and be prepared to explain their rating
• Consider the influence of circumstances, beliefs and feelings on decisions and events	Learners compete to list all the different influences caused by children's belief in Father Christmas on families, advertisers, retailers, television schedulers and performers. The list can be extended and divided so that small groups of learners consider the effect on different types of people
• Support conclusions, using reasoned arguments and evidence	Give each learner a short article from a newspaper about, for example, a trial or a music event. Ask them to draw a conclusion about: • the character of a main person or performer at the trial or event • why the crime or event happened. Ask learners to compare and justify their conclusion to a partner or a small group

These are also the skills that will support learners in developing the other transferable skills already described in this chapter such as employability and enterprise skills, wider key skills and PLTS.

Functional skills will replace the key skills of communication, application of number and ICT. These qualifications are designed for learners over the age of 16 who have left compulsory full-time education and who do not have up-to-date English, mathematics or ICT qualifications at level 2. Some schools have offered Skills for Life (sometimes referred to as Basic Skills) qualifications to 14–16 year olds.

Functional English

Functional English covers the speaking and listening, reading and writing skills that will be needed by learners in a range of contexts and for different purposes to understand and communicate with other people. These skills include:

- Making active contributions to discussions
- Reading and understanding a range of texts
- Writing documents for different purposes.

Functional mathematics

Functional mathematics covers the process skills that enable learners to do the following:

- Understand a situation
- Choose an approach to tackle the problem
- Formulate a model using mathematics
- Use mathematics to provide answers
- Interpret and check the result
- Evaluate the model and approach
- Explain the analysis and results.

Functional ICT

Functional ICT expects learners to be capable of using ICT techniques to produce solutions to problems, within different routines and contexts. Learners also need to understand the role ICT plays in the world at large. The skills include:

- Using ICT systems
- Finding and selecting information
- Developing, presenting and communicating information.

Differentiating between levels of skills

Functional skills standards are currently available for entry level to level 2 and learners' work is currently accredited through an external assessment. Differentiation between the levels is determined by the following factors.

The *complexity* of situations and activities
Learners need to be able to identify the different steps needed to complete a task or solve a problem. Booking a studio for editing is a more straightforward task than carrying out a health and safety recce for filming at an outside location.

A learner's level of *familiarity* with the task or activity
Learners need to be able to transfer the understanding and skills they use on a daily basis in familiar surroundings to situations with which they are less familiar. Learners will usually be familiar with participating in a production meeting with their peers but may struggle to contribute to staff meetings held at a work placement.

The *technical demand* associated with these activities
Learners need a wide range of generic knowledge, skills and techniques to handle different situations or problems. They should recognize which 'tools' they will need to use and apply them in different contexts. It is hard to imagine a 14+ learner who has not used ICT; however, their knowledge and skills may be patchy. For example, a performing arts learner may have good skills in word processing but be unable to select and use software applications that manipulate graphics and allow them to produce effective publicity.

The level of *independence* with which a learner can complete the activity
As learners progress through the levels, they will demonstrate their independence through being able to select and demonstrate appropriate functional skills and techniques confidently and without always needing full support from others. Learners can be motivated to achieve functional skills if they are embedded in their vocational programme. This enables them to see the relevance of acquiring these skills and provides them with the opportunities to practise the skills in a vocational setting. However, creative arts and media teachers should not be expected to have total responsibility for delivering the functional English, mathematics and ICT knowledge, skills and techniques unless they are functional skills experts. Learners are also expected to be able to transfer their skills to a range of contexts so if they only practise them within creative arts and media, they may not be prepared for a summative external assessment that has tasks related to other vocational areas and life experiences.

Using various functional skills

Box 3.1 gives an example of an assignment brief that provides learners with the opportunity to demonstrate their functional skills by addressing a real-life problem in a vocational context.

Box 3.1 Marketing research assignment

You are marketing a new theatre performance (media product or art exhibition) for a client. The client is particularly interested in the type of audience that should be targeted and the type of publicity that will appeal to them. You will need to carry out research on how similar performances are successfully marketed. This research will be done through interviews or focus groups as well as using newspapers, books, magazines and the Internet.

The client expects you to evaluate the information and make a presentation at their next meeting with you. The client expects you to suggest which publicity will be most successful in attracting a large audience. At this meeting a written report should be also presented which includes statistics on the potential audience.

Table 3.3 identifies the opportunities in this assignment for using functional skills.

Table 3.3 Opportunities for using functional skills

Level 2 Speaking and listening
- Carry out interviews and focus groups with potential audience members
- Make a presentation to a client and suggest ideas for publicity
- Lead an informal discussion with members of a focus group
- Respond formally to questions from the client
- Carry out roles as an interviewer and a presenter to reach decisions on the type of audience and publicity needed for a new performance

Level 2 Reading
- Analyse marketing material such as newspaper theatre reviews, magazine publicity articles on actors, posters
- Read information about the performance to be marketed
- Extract information from these materials for the written report and to use in the presentation

Level 2 Writing
- Structure information within the written report
- Summarize research materials for the report
- Make accurate written notes during interviews and focus groups
- Handwrite interview notes to capture the gist of discussions
- Make an initial draft of the report
- Use formal language in the report
- Make brief written notes for the verbal presentation
- Word process, proofread and amend the written report

Level 2 Mathematics
- Understand box office figures and relate these to a potential future audience for a new theatre performance
- Estimate the number of words in the written report
- Count the number of similar responses to interview questions
- Convert box office percentages into fractions when presenting statistical data in the presentation
- Present audience statistics from Internet research in the written report, using tables, pi-charts or graphs
- Interpret statistics in a written form for the client

Level 2: Use ICT systems
- Use the computer to carry out research, word process notes and write the report
- Use a broadband connection to carry out web searches
- Word process the report, use graphics to present data
- Use the scrollbar when scanning web pages for information
- Use a template to write the report
- Create folders to store research material and drafts of the report
- Print the report
- Save the report on a memory stick
- Check that cables from a laptop do not trip other people
- Use a wrist rest when producing the report
- Make a backup of your files
- Treat any information sent to you in an email attachment with caution
- Respect confidentiality when saving interview notes
- Report any virus threat when carrying out research via the Internet
- Know which technician can deal with paper jams or other printing problems

Level 2: Find and select information
- Find information about audiences and types of publicity for theatre performances from newspapers, books, images, conversations, websites and podcasts
- Acknowledge ownership of any existing publicity material included in the written report
- Recognize that some interviewees may not want their names to be included in the report
- Avoid plagiarism by summarizing information and acknowledging sources
- Enter web addresses, use a search engine, browse, save and use bookmarks when carrying out Internet research
- Use multiple search criteria such as audiences, theatre performances and marketing to locate appropriate information
- Use current information that is related only to theatre audiences rather than television audiences

Level 2: Develop, present and communicate information
- Use a template and include headings, subheadings, lists and tables in the report
- Edit the report to sequence information logically
- Set margins and number pages in the report
- Use bullet points and adjust font style and size to improve the legibility of the report and make it look attractive

(Continued overleaf)

Table 3.3 Continued.

- Add borders or shading to tables to make them easier to read and understand
- Include examples of publicity such as posters and actors' photographs in the report
- Include a logo of your 'company' at the top of the report
- Include charts and graphs showing audience statistics in the report
- Use a scattergram to show different ideas for publicity in the report
- Use text boxes in the report to contain quotes from interviewees
- Use captions under images of publicity in the report
- Check spelling in the report, use print preview to check that the layout is consistent
- Produce the report in an accepted format

Delivering functional skills effectively

Many creative arts and media learners do not achieve the grades they hope for because they are let down by ineffective research, individual monitoring of the production process and presentation of work. These are all issues that can be addressed through effective delivery of functional skills.

Reports by chief examiners, moderators and coordinators for creative arts and media programmes often identify the weaknesses listed below. As you read the list, reflect on how these might be addressed with support from a functional skills teacher.

Areas for improvement in learner evidence include the following:

- Misunderstanding of the assignment brief resulting in weak responses
- Limited use of research methods, especially face-to-face or other verbal research, for instance lack of effective questioning skills
- Inability to summarize research (unannotated downloads are included)
- Inability to gain detailed audience or consumer feedback
- Lack of evaluation of the research sources in terms of currency, bias and so on
- Superficial, inaccurate or retrospective notes recording planning, production and performance processes
- Lack of recognition of appropriate writing styles, for example commercial style reviews rather than personal critical responses, or reports that are subjective rather than objective, inclusion of contact details on business type documents such as proposals and reports
- Report format not understood and reports that read like essays
- Poor layout or work resulting in a lack of clarity, such as insufficient use of headings, subheadings and paragraphs
- Weak grammar and spelling not only in supporting documentation but also in end products such as posters, electronic presentation slides, video titling, newspaper or magazine articles, questionnaires

- Creative work not addressing an intended audience, consumer or client appropriately
- Illogical sequencing of evidence in portfolios
- Superficial understanding of funding and inaccurate budgets and estimates
- Lack of understanding of scheduling
- Inability to interpret data including statistics
- Weak interpretation and poor presentation of statistics in charts and graphs
- Poor presentation of images in written work, for example blurring, over-sized, misplaced
- Unedited audio or video recordings, lacking transcripts
- Electronic presentations with too much information on the slides
- Lack of ability to talk about presentation slides clearly
- Evidence of plagiarism; sources and quotes not acknowledged
- Insufficient labelling of work
- Evidence difficult to locate because of lack of pagination and indexing
- Inclusion of early drafts rather than final work.

Reflection 3.4

- How can collaboration between creative arts and media teachers and functional skills staff be improved?
- How effectively do induction activities support initial assessment of learners' functional skills?
- How confident are you in embedding functional skills into your creative arts and media programme and how can a whole organizational approach to embedding functional skills support you?

In this chapter, we have discussed the wider skills agenda and identified skills that learners need to enable them to function in employment in the creative and media industries, be effective citizens and lifelong learners. With the rate of change brought about by the electronic age and globalization, acquiring knowledge is not enough. Learners need the skills to be able to respond to new and novel situations and sometimes to generate new knowledge to enable them to succeed.

References

1   Leitch Report (2006) *Leitch Review of Skills: Prosperity for All in the Global Economy – World-Class Skills*. The National Archives and HM Treasury. Available from: http://webarchive.nationalarchives.gov.uk/+/www.hm-treasury.gov.uk/leitch [Accessed 22 July 2010].
2   Institute of Directors (IOD) (2007). Available from: www.iod.com/Home/Policy/Education-and-Skills/Briefing-Papers/Briefing-Paper—-Skills-and-Training/ [Accessed 22 July 2010].

3   Excellence Gateway. Available from: http://tlp.excellencegateway.org.uk/tlp/cam/resource/
    html/enterprise_cam.php [Accessed 23 July 2010].
4   Department for Education. *Functional Skills*. Available from: www.fssupport.org/resources
    [Accessed 23 July 2010].
5   Gantt chart. Available from: http://gantt.com/index.htm [Accessed 23 July 2010].

Further reading

Davies, P. and Brant, J. (2006) *Business, Economics and Enterprise: Teaching School Subjects
    11–19*. London: Routledge.
Harmer, J. (2007) *The Practice of English Language Teaching*, 4th edn. Harlow: Pearson
    Longman.
Hind, D.W.G. and Moss, S. (2005) *Employability Skills*. Sunderland: Business Education.
Information about personal, learning and thinking skills (PLTS) can be found at: www.teach-
    ingexpertise.com/e-bulletins/implementing-qcas-framework-for-plts-personal-learning-
    and-thinking-skills-3087 [Accessed 23 July 2010].

4

Essential creative arts and media skills

By the end of this chapter, you will be able to:

- Support your learners in creating exciting and feasible ideas
- Explain how to carry out purposeful and effective research
- Develop your learners' team building and project management skills

Introduction

The following four sets of skills (ideas generation, research, team building and project management) are also transferable skills but they are so important for creative arts and media learners that they have a chapter to themselves. The chapter begins with an exploration of what is meant by a 'new idea' and how learners can evaluate their ideas. This is followed by a section on research, its purposes and the range of research methods that learners can employ, including questionnaires, interviews, focus groups and print and web-based research. There is guidance on how to reference source material. The final section looks at team building, its roles and processes and the project management skills that creative arts and media learners need.

Ideas generation

What is an idea?

All creative and media industries are constantly on the lookout for new ideas so that they can attract new audiences or consumers and maintain the interest of current audiences and consumers. It is, however, rare for an idea to be completely new and learners sometimes do not recognize this. They struggle to find some unique and original 'flash of inspiration'.

A 'new' idea could be related to:

- Content, for example the storyline in a novel, the dance steps in a ballet, the fabric used in a fashion garment
- Treatment, for example the humour given to a television documentary, the use of space helmets as headgear in a fashion show
- A product or performance targeted at a different audience *or* group of consumers, such as a portrait exhibition aimed at children instead of adults
- Not for a whole new product or performance but for a partial change, for example the stage set for a Shakespearian play is changed to a different period, a different presenter of a quiz show is introduced, or the colour and style of the masthead of a newspaper is subtly altered.

Once learners start to think in terms of the type and scope of the ideas they want to develop, they can begin looking for the 'flash of inspiration'. Inspiration might come from real events, people, social issues, political issues, sequels, remakes, spin-offs and influences from other media, products, performances, fashion shows, exhibitions, paintings, sculpture, music, moods and the senses; touch (texture), sight (colour), sound, smell, taste, and other less tangible things such as the seasons, language, ethics and philosophy, the works of great artists, designers, musicians, performers and producers.

Reflection 4.1

- Are there some sources of inspiration your learners might neglect?
- Who or what has been your greatest source of inspiration and why?
- To what extent are you personally an inspiration for your learners?

Evaluating ideas

Sometimes learners can come up with ideas that are too wild and beyond their ability and resources to produce. Other learners might worry that their ideas are not daring or different enough. You may need to remind learners about why the creative and media industries take forward ideas. Learners might use the following list as criteria to evaluate their own ideas.

An idea will be developed if it

- makes money
- satisfies a public demand or need
- fills a gap in the market
- is topical
- is seasonal
- is commemorative

- is shocking
- is aesthetic
- appeals to a mass audience
- follows a trend
- satisfies the demand for a sequel or spin-off
- takes a fresh look at a popular old idea
- is a vehicle for a star
- is suitable for spawning merchandising.

Assessing feasibility of ideas

Learners can sometimes forget that their own ideas must be feasible. They can become demotivated and disengaged if they try to produce a product or performance that is too big or long or too complex. They should always consider feasibility in terms of:

- *Cost,* for example even a school or college production should have a budget and learners should always be encouraged to include in budgeting, professional rates for the time they spend working in a particular role. This will prepare them for the world of work.
- *Time,* for example is there enough time to plan, research, rehearse and carry out a final performance or make a media product or artefact in the sessions available?
- *Human resource,* for example are there enough people in their team to cover all the work? To what extent can they access technical support or advice from a teacher, client or industry mentor?
- *Location,* for example which areas can they film, rehearse, hold meetings or perform in? What permissions are needed?
- *Equipment and materials,* for example will there be enough equipment such as cameras, lighting or materials such as paint and fabric to realize ideas?

Reflection 4.2

- To what extent do your learners evaluate their ideas in terms of profitability and feasibility?
- What types of research do your learners carry out to test their ideas?
- Which local creative professionals might be prepared to speak to your learners about ideas generation and creativity?

Box 4.1 describes how an idea for a new print product was developed. The feasibility criteria above are in bold in the text. You might work with a creative professional or use your own experience as an industry professional to produce a local case study to use with learners.

Box 4.1 Producing an advertising magazine

Alex saw a niche in the free newspaper market in his area. Manufacturers, retailers and people offering specialist services could advertise in the existing local newspaper, the regional newspaper and a tabloid-sized newspaper delivered free to every household in the area. The problem for advertisers with all of these was that people seldom read them all the way through and would throw them away quickly, therefore missing their adverts.

Alex decided to produce the *Newtown Advertiser*, a free A5 magazine full of advertisements that people could keep by the telephone. Advertisers soon found that sales figures rose significantly after they had placed an advert in this publication.

Costs were kept to a minimum by having no editorial copy and no news stories. There were two reasons for this. First, there was no journalist or photographer to pay. Second, advertisers would not be offended by any editorial or political stance that they might disagree with. It was printed on good quality paper (90gm), but the only colour used was on the front cover so that householders could quickly spot it lying on a table or by the telephone.

Alex had sufficient **time** to produce copies of the magazine every month. Advertisers would send in copy over a period of three weeks and it would take one week to do the page layout, print and package the magazines ready for distribution.

The company had the **human resources**. The production of the publication required only the equivalent of three full-time members of staff. Alex was responsible for the printing but another member of staff, Juliette, was responsible for selling advertising space, meeting clients and designing the page layout. Part-time members of staff did telesales and the accounts. In addition, the company hired a distribution team.

In terms of **equipment and materials**, the company already had a computer running Corel-Draw and Photoshop, a scanner, supplies of paper, an Oki Laser printer for running off the draft copy onto film, a machine to transfer the film onto plates and a printing press.

The first editions of the publication were used to test the market and distributed in a small **location** to 6,000 homes. The success of the *Newtown Advertiser* soon meant that the run was increased to 7,000 and editions to cover other local areas were planned. The first one of these was the *Old Village Advertiser*, which was distributed to 15,000 homes.

Alex soon realized that the popularity with advertisers meant that he could charge more for advertising space. This would make the publication more financially viable. For example, the cost of a full page advert (128mm × 190mm) was raised from £105 for a single insertion in the original *Newtown Advertiser* to £130 in the *Old Village* edition and to £200 in the latest *Bigtown* edition (because of its larger circulation).

> **Reflection 4.3**
>
> - What other factors might learners consider when evaluating ideas, for example legal constraints such as copyright, censorship, and ethical constraints such as privacy or decency or competition from other products?
> - How often do your learners have the opportunity to present their ideas to a client?
> - How might you involve business experts in helping learners evaluate their ideas?

You might like to direct your learners to websites such as the BBC's New Talent Showcase (www.bbc.co.uk/newtalent/) or the BBC's Performing Arts Fund website (www.bbc.co.uk/performingartsfund/) which are particularly helpful in encouraging young people develop their ideas.

First Film Foundation (www.firstfilm.co.uk/) helps new writers, producers and directors to make their first feature film. It helps them to forge links with the established film industry and gives impartial and practical advice on how to develop a career in the film industry. The Foundation runs programmes that take new filmmakers from development through to production and exhibition. It provides opportunities for new filmmakers to have their scripts reviewed, enter competitions and showcase their work.

Working with clients

To progress their ideas, creative and media people usually need to work with a client – someone with the finance and resources to take a new idea to the next stage. The client could be a theatrical impresario, a television company, the owner of an art gallery, a publisher or a manufacturing or retail company. The client may be a commissioning editor of a large organization such as a book publisher or a private individual who wants photographs taken of their wedding.

It is important that learners have the opportunities to present their ideas in the most professional way either through writing documents such as proposals and treatments or business plans. For example, a proposal and treatment for an enterprise, creative arts or media product or service will include information such as the following:

- Contact details of the person with the idea
- Name of the venture
- The date the proposal is sent
- Basic idea or concept
- The genre
- The format (including details such as length, size, type of tape or electronic recording format, quality of paper, number of pages, as appropriate to the medium)
- The purpose
- Profile of the target audience or consumer

- The unique selling point (USP) and what makes this idea different
- A summary of audience research that justifies the ideas: it will explain how the new product meets the specific needs of a group of readers, viewers, listeners or gamers. This research may also give statistical information on current or potential audiences or consumers. It may be based on opinions given in a focus group or feedback from interviews with individual members of the audience or consumer group.
- If possible a list of other work in this area and a summary of any critical reviews, sales figures and so on
- Assets, such as you and your team members' personal qualities and skills, qualifications, facilities, equipment and materials.

Some creative and media proposals will include in a treatment:

- Detailed description of content and structure
- Sample materials (e.g. drafts, storyboards, suggested page layout, sample copy, section of a script) or a showreel
- Schedule for production.

Proposals and business plans should be word processed and presented to give a professional image. If the creative and media company provides a proforma for proposals and treatments or guidelines on how to present them, then these should be used. It is essential that the written documents and sample materials such as showreels or sample chapters of a book provide a clear picture of the intended product or performance and give accurate information.

> **Reflection 4.4**
>
> - What opportunities do you offer to learners to work with different types of clients?
> - What functional skills will support learners in working with clients?
> - How might it benefit learners to work with other learners on business programmes?

Research

The purpose of research

Learners need to be clear why they are carrying out research. Is it to find content for a product or performance, assess the market or investigate potential consumers or audiences? A common error for some learners is to make research too general. Others carry out the research but forget to analyse the results and draw conclusions. Even learners who present their findings effectively, can then forget to use their research to influence their own work.

Audience and consumer research

Research needs to be done on the content of the creative and media products and performances that are being created, but research also needs to take place on the interests and needs of the potential audiences and consumers of the creative and media products. Audience and consumer research might include:

- The audience or consumer profile
- Size of the potential audience or consumer group
- Market competition
- Marketing strategies.

Even level 3 learners will quite often state that their product or performance is for 'everybody' and they may seem quite unaware of the extent to which the creative and media industries carry out research. Audience and consumer profiles can be constructed in a number of ways, for example through demographic and socio-economic research or psychographic profiling.

Demographic and socio-economic research

Demographic and socio-economic research divides people into different groupings such as age, class, gender, financial background, and the area where they live. Table 4.1 gives examples of occupations and their social grade.

One regional newspaper used Table 4.1 to classify its readers. It found out that of people in the area who bought newspapers, 15 per cent were AB readers, 25 per cent were C1 readers, 28 per cent were C2 readers and 32 per cent were DE readers. This influenced the style and length of news articles, the topics covered and the vocabulary used in the articles.

The classification shown in Table 4.1, though still used, is becoming less useful in the twenty-first century where patterns of employment and types of job are more diverse.

Table 4.1 Social grades and occupations

Social grade	Description of occupation	Example
A	Higher management and administrative staff or professionals	Company director
B	Intermediate management and administrative staff or professionals	Middle management
C1	Supervisory, clerical, junior management and administrative staff or professionals	Bank clerk
C2	Skilled manual workers	Plumber
D	Semiskilled and unskilled manual workers	Labourer
E	State pensioners with no income, widows, casual and lowest grade earners	Unemployed

Psychographic profiling

Psychographic profiling cuts across socio-economic and demographic boundaries and includes lifestyle groupings. It is concerned with how individuals see themselves and what they want to be like. It classifies them according to their interests, opinions, beliefs and values. For example, a 16-year-old female and a 60-year-old male may be in the same grouping if they both aspire to travel the world though one may be affluent and the other unemployed.

Cross Cultural Consumer Characterization

One example of a lifestyle classification model is that developed by Young and Rubicam, the Cross Cultural Consumer Characterization (4Cs).[1] It divides the population into the following main groups:

- Mainstreamers like to conform and be secure
- Aspirers want material success and novelties
- Succeeders have status and like control
- Reformers are well educated and interested in social issues
- Explorers are independent, adventurous and welcome challenges
- Resigned are traditional, strict and value economy and safety
- Strugglers may be disorganized and have unhealthy lifestyles.

MOSAIC

The MOSAIC lifestyle groupings system is popular worldwide with advertisers and defines 12 groups consisting of people who share a number of characteristics.[2] For example, the characteristics of STYLISH SINGLES are that they are typically well educated, tend to be non-conformist, highly interested in people from other social groups and enjoy living in a cosmopolitan or multicultural environment. They live busy lives and may delay getting married, having children or buying their own home. They spend a lot on eating out, fashion, travel, the arts and entertainment. They are typically aged between 25 and 34 and live in rented flats. Examples like this might help learners gain a more sophisticated approach to audience or consumer research.

Types of research

Learners should be able to carry out market research and content research and both quantitative and qualitative research. They should be encouraged to carry out more than one type of research. Methods include:

- Questionnaires
- In-depth interviews
- Focus groups
- Observation groups

- Print and web-based research
- Collection of materials.

You might compile a list of research tasks that can be carried out quickly and whose purpose is clear. Some examples are given in Table 4.2.

Table 4.2 Examples of research tasks

What is the project?	What needs to be researched?	Research methods
Putting on a fashion show for college work	What is the best time for the fashion show so that adults can attend?	Questionnaire carried out in the local schools, college and library
Compiling a photographic exhibition	Where would be the best place for it to be seen to maximum effect by teenagers?	Interviewing a professional photographer
Producing a new magazine on owning pets	The type of animal to put on the front page that will attract readers	Focus group with magazine readers who have pets

Reflection 4.5

- When preparing a scheme of work, is enough time allocated to research and development? Is time put on one side to review the findings of the research and relate this back to the finished piece of work?
- Do your learners use a range of research skills or stick to one or two types, for example the Internet or mood boards? Do they do what they like to do rather than what is most appropriate?
- Do your learners have an environment suitable for carrying out research? Can they go out into a town to carry out a questionnaire? Do they have access to a quiet room to carry out interviews?

Questionnaires

Learners need to be aware of why questionnaires are used for research, how they are constructed and how the data are collected and analysed.

A questionnaire is an example of quantitative research and the people who fill in questionnaires are known as respondents. It answers questions like 'How many?' rather than 'Why?' This produces statistical information. A questionnaire usually asks closed questions. The answer will usually be a 'Yes' or a 'No' or respondents to the questionnaire will tick boxes. An example of a closed question is 'Do you buy a daily newspaper?'

Questionnaires are fairly inexpensive to run and analyse. They can be used with a large sample of people. Many people like answering questionnaires, because they are usually anonymous. However, it is essential that the questions are easy to answer and are unambiguous. The results can be analysed by computer and presented as graphs and diagrams. The data are then interpreted to give broad conclusions. A weakness of questionnaires is that only simple questions can be asked and only the most sophisticated type of questionnaires are constructed with checks to see if questions are answered honestly and correctly. Learners will often underestimate the time it takes to design even a simple questionnaire.

Box 4.2 contains a few questions extracted from a professional questionnaire run by a large regional newspaper company given to its readers. Note the format of the questions and the detail. Why do you think these questions were asked? You might simplify, extend or contextualize this to use as an example with performing arts or art and design learners.

Box 4.2 Items from a questionnaire for newspaper readers

Q1   Besides our newspaper, is there another newspaper you read regularly? Which is it?

Q2   How long do you spend reading (NAME OF NEWSPAPER)?

Less than 5 minutes	About 5 minutes	About 10 minutes
About 15 minutes	About 20 minutes	About 25 minutes
About 30 minutes	About 35 minutes	About 40 minutes
About 45 minutes	About 1 hour	About 1¼ hours
About 1¾ hours	About 2 hours	More than 2 hours
Don't know		

Q2   And how much of the most recent issue of our newspaper did you read?

All of it	Most of it	About half of it
Less than half of it	Very little of it	Don't know

Q3   Which days of the week do you normally read (NAME OF NEWSPAPER)?

Monday	Tuesday	Wednesday
Thursday	Friday	Saturday
Sunday		

Q4   What would you say are your main reasons for reading (NAME OF NEWSPAPER) on (DAY SPECIFIED AT Q3 ABOVE)?

Local news	Local issues
Jobs	Property
Classified ads	What's on
Motors	Family announcements
Sport	TV pages
Other	(please specify)
Anything else?	

Q5   Which one of the above sections would you turn to first?

....

Q6   Look at the following list of statements that people have made about their local newspapers. Tick which statements you think particularly apply to (NAME OF NEWSPAPER)

Has a strong personality	You can lose yourself in it
Is thought provoking	Provides balanced and objective coverage
Has a lot of information but is not for me	Is good value for money
Is an essential part of my day	Reflects my values
Is boring	Captures the mood (of the region)
Speaks with authority	You can talk about it with other people
Is not relevant to me	Is campaigning and gets things done
Reveals facts ordinary people have a right to know	

In-depth interviews

Learners can be reluctant to conduct the in-depth interviews that are excellent for carrying out qualitative research but can be time consuming.[3] Time must be allocated not only for doing the interview but also for analysing and presenting the information. The main error in interviewing is when learners do not spend enough time in preparing for the interview. This type of research is often used to find out about emotions, opinions and attitudes so interviewees should be encouraged to give longer responses by being asked open questions which ask for reasons or descriptions, rather than closed questions that usually encourage 'Yes' or 'No' answers. An example of an open question would be 'Why do you only visit the theatre once a year?' Learners need practice in order to be professional and friendly and encourage the interviewee to be open. However, they may find this difficult if they only have opportunities to interview members of their peer group.

Learners need to be aware that organizing interviews includes the following decisions:

1   What is the focus of the interview?
2   Who will be interviewed?
3   When will the interviews take place?
4   How long will the interviews last?
5   Where will the interviews take place?
6   Will the interviews be formal or informal?
7   What general questions will be asked to set the interviewee at ease?

8   How will I explain what the interview is about?

9   What open-ended question will be asked to find detailed information?

10   What prompt or follow-up questions are needed?

11   Will I let the interviewee see the key question beforehand?

12   How will the information be recorded?

Reflection 4.6

- How often do your learners practise their interviewing techniques through role-play?

- What exemplar material do you show learners, demonstrating good interviewing skills, e.g. a chat show host, mock job interviews.

- What local creative and media professionals do you know who would be prepared to be interviewed by learners?

Focus groups

Focus groups are excellent for carrying out qualitative research.[4] A typical focus group will consist of between five and ten people, who will talk informally about their needs for a new product or their use of a product. It might equally be used for audiences to talk about their impressions of a film preview or theatrical dress rehearsal. A typical focus group is highly structured. It lasts for about two hours and is run by a moderator who guides the conversation and focuses the group on the topic to be discussed. Too small a group and the discussion may be limited in its scope, too large a group and people may feel inhibited to express themselves. A focus group may be better for learners to carry out than individual interviews because people are less self-conscious when talking in a group and it is easier for you as a teacher to observe and assess or to role-play the focus group moderator.

In the creative and media industries, the people in the focus group will have been chosen because they represent the type of person who will belong to the target audience or consumer group of the new product or performance. Researchers should not choose people who are too close such as friends or relatives. The members of a focus group will sit together in a relaxed atmosphere and chat informally about different products and services directly or indirectly related to what is being researched. However, the researcher usually will direct the conversation and guide the group onto relevant topics. Sample material such as a magazine article or a television advert is usually handed out as a stimulus and sufficient time must be given for the group to read, watch or listen to such material. Usually these sessions are videoed or taped to make recording data and analysis easier. It is very difficult to follow several people talking at once and write down what each says as well as observe their body language.

Read the publicity in Box 4.3 for a company that runs focus groups. Identify how your learners can mirror the working practices of the company.

Box 4.3 Publicity for a company running focus groups

Who are we?

Creative Focus PLC is a top facility for offering a complete qualitative market re-search service including focus groups. We have organized focus groups for a wide range of products and services including mobile phone companies, newspapers and advertisers. We do not initiate research but you the client can use us to carry out your research. For example, a newspaper company wanted to find out if it should change format from broadsheet to tabloid. We were able to find the respondents and a moderator and arrange the time and place for the sessions.

How do we organize the focus group?

Creative Focus PLC has a large database with over 10,000 names from which we can find respondents who live within reach of the M25 (London orbital motorway) and therefore have easy access to London. These names are screened to find an appropri-ate group, e.g. females aged 20–30. Only about 1 in 23 will match the screening and be able to attend the focus group on a particular day. Creative Focus PLC staff usually talk to about 200 people in order to find the eight who will be part of the focus group. Respondents will be paid a fee, the amount depending on the length of the session and how special they are and how valuable their time is. For example, for a typical two-hour session, a teenager may receive £35, an urban professional £50–60, executives and wealthy people between £80 and £150. Generally focus groups are run in the evening from 6 to 8 p.m. and from 8 to 10 p.m.

Who will carry out the session?

The moderator may work for a research company or be freelance. Sometimes they can be academics.

Jasper, our studio manager, says: 'Our moderators are good with people, flexible, open-minded, quick to learn and observant. They are objective and able to report clearly the results to you the client even if those results are not what you want to hear!'

What are the facilities?

Depending on the group, focus sessions can be held in different types of rooms:
- A formal room with a conference style table and chairs
- An informal room with comfy chairs around a coffee table to mimic a living room.

The respondents are given refreshments that can vary from sandwiches to a hot buffet.

It is usual for our moderators to use a stimulus to promote conversation, so the rooms are equipped with LCD projectors, laptops and flipcharts so that respondents can be shown video or audio clips or diagrams. To assess the effectiveness of an advertising campaign, storyboards and 30 second rough cuts of adverts are shown to respondents to gauge their reactions. Another popular technique is to bring in magazines. Respondents cut out any images they might associate with a product and a collage is made.

What data are collected?

Although a moderator might note that five out of eight people liked the product, the data collected is qualitative rather than statistical because the sample of eight people is so small. The important thing is for the moderator to find out why the product is liked or how it is used. The sessions are recorded on video and audio. To meet legal and ethical requirements as given by the Market Research Society and to comply with laws on privacy and personal information, respondents are made aware of this at the start of the session.

Observation groups

Observation groups are frequently used to research products for young children, such as toys. Such research is also carried out to watch the effects of media products such as television programmes on children. When the observation is *covert*, the subjects are unaware that they are being watched. When the observation is *overt*, the researcher explains who they are and possibly why they are watching.

Learners might consider running an observation group if they have made a children's animation or written a children's book. Learners might also use this type of research to find out how audience behaviour might affect the content of performance, exhibition or a media product. For example, they might observe a friend or family member when they are watching the television. Do they talk during the programme? Do they leave the room while the programme is on? Are they doing something else while watching the programme such as eating or their homework? Do they channel hop? You might ask learners to draw some conclusions about what parts of the programme attract them to it and keep their attention, such as the theme tune, a scene with action, the end cliff-hanging sequence.

Print and web-based research and collection of materials

These days, creative arts and media professionals can carry out extensive research without leaving their desks and access a wide range of sources including film and picture archives or news agencies, though some of these will expect payment. Artists and designers also collate large collections of materials such as sample textiles, drawings or natural materials that will inspire them in future projects.

When asked to research, most learners will turn to the Internet and occasionally books, magazines, audio and video materials, or collect images from magazines or samples of textiles to create collages. The main weaknesses in carrying out and using this kind of research are:

- The research is too unfocused
- Research is limited to one or two websites
- Sources are not cited properly or materials are not logged
- A lack of awareness of which information is in the public domain and which is restricted or covered by copyright legislation
- The information is not summarized (downloads are included)
- The information or materials are poorly organized or indexed
- The information is not analysed
- The information is not evaluated for accuracy, reliability or currency.

Reflection 4.7

- Which of the weaknesses listed above do you recognize in your learners' research?
- How often do you use support from information specialists (e.g. librarians) to deliver sessions on research?
- What strategies might you use to prevent plagiarism, e.g. accept only summaries.

Writing a bibliography or compiling references

Learners should be aware of the importance of citing sources or quoting references so that:

- The originators of the source material are acknowledged
- Readers of their work can check the accuracy and currency of information
- Readers of their work can locate the source material themselves.

The examples below are based on the Harvard (author-date) method. Other methods (e.g. author-title or numbered references) can be used; what is important is that any method is used consistently.

Below are some examples of references that might be included at the end of a creative arts and media project portfolio or in a research log.

Books
(Note that the book titles are given in italics.)
Dawkins, S. and Wynd, I. (2010) *Video Production: Putting Theory into Practice.* Basingstoke: Palgrave Macmillan.
Thornton, S. (2006) Understanding hipness, in A. Bennett, B. Shank and J. Toynbee (eds) *Popular Music Studies Reader.* London: Routledge.
The Writers' & Artists' Yearbook 2010 (2010) London: A & C Black.
(Note that the above book is an example of multiple authorship. Other examples include encyclopaedias, dictionaries and anthologies. If there is an editor, his or her name should be included, as shown below.)

Jensen, K.B. (ed.) (2002) *A Handbook of Media and Communication Research: Qualitative and Quantitative Methodologies*. London: Routledge.

Magazines, journals and newspapers
(Note that the title of the magazine, journal or newspaper is given in italics; '205–208' and '491–512' refer to the page numbers.)

Sinclair, C. (2008) Top of the box: Dressing for TV is riddled with pitfalls. *Vogue*, November, 205–208.
Thompson, E. and Laing, A. (2003) The net generation: Children and young people, the Internet and online shopping. *Journal of Marketing Management*, 19(3–4): 491–512.
(If the article has no byline, i.e. a journalist's or correspondent's name is not attached, repeat the publication's name as the author.)
The Times (2010) Artist loses fight to halt charges. *The Times*, 27 March, 53.
(The '53' refers to the page number.)

CD-ROMs and DVDs
Mr. Bean's Holiday (2007) Film. Directed by Steve Bendelack. UK: Universal Pictures.
Middlemarch (2001) DVD. BBC Worldwide.
Florence + the Machine (2009) *Lungs*. CD-ROM. Universal Island Records.

(Note it can be difficult sometimes to state a country as music can be recorded in one country but the label may be based in another and owned by a multinational. Referencing music DVDs can be a good way to initiate discussion with learners on ownership and copyright.)

Broadcasts
Tropic of Cancer, Episode 3, 2010. TV, BBC2, 28 March 2010.
Requests with Jamie Crick, 2010. Radio, Classic FM, 1 April 2010.

Online materials (e.g. web pages, blogs, moving images, podcasts)
Creative Choices. *A Career in Advertising*. Available from: www.creative-choices.co. uk/knowledge/a-career-in. . ./a-career-in-advertising . . . [Accessed 1 April 2010].
Skills North East. *ICT and Digital Media Sector Report*. Available from: www.skills northeast.co.uk/lib/liDownload/14707/ICT%20and%20Dig%20Media%20-%20 FINAL.pdf?CFID=9534493&CFTOKEN=98516555 [Accessed 1 April 2010].
British Pathe Archive. *The Evolution of the Film*. Available from: www.britishpathe. com/record.php?id=14505 [Accessed 1 April 2010].
The Academy BLOG. *Inspired by the Ancient Greeks*. Available from: http://blog. theacademyarts.com/ [Accessed 1 April 2010].
YouTube. *Interview with Julian Casablancas, 2010*. Available from www.youtube.com/ watch?v—_rB8GD_z-Q&feature=fvhl [Accessed 1 April 2010].
(Note that it is usual to state when online materials were accessed. For research logs, this could also be done for paper-based materials, i.e. when they were used by the learner.)

Photographs, paintings, sculptures, performances, exhibitions
Lanford Wilson (1970) Play, *Serenading Louie*, performed by Donmar Warehouse,
    director Simon Curtis, The Curve Leicester, 10 April 2010.
Mario Testino (1996) Photograph, *Naomi Campbell*, National Portrait Gallery, London.
Henry Moore, Sculpture exhibition, Tate Britain, 24 February 2010.

Team building

Most creative and media employees will at some time work as part of a team (which
may consist of two or three people as in a design company or hundreds as in film
production) so learners need to understand how effective teams are formed.
    Job roles can be considered to fall into three categories:

* Decision-making roles such as a manager, director or editor
* Practitioner roles that demand specific technical or creative skills such as a camera
  operator, graphic designer, script writer or dancer
* Support roles such as financial or administrative staff.

Learners should appreciate that within a team some members may have discrete
roles, such as camera operator or computer programmer, but in other teams, members
will be expected to multitask and that sometimes freelance workers such as designers
or producers are brought into a team to work with permanent staff on a particular
project. An effective team regardless of size will require a diversity of specific and
transferable skills, personal qualities and roles.

Team roles

A researcher at the Henley Centre, Dr Meredith Belbin, identified nine sets of characteristics that form distinct team roles.[5] Any team is not complete without all of
them. He thought that when people select team members, they choose either people
like themselves or ones they find it easy to relate to, rather than those that complement
each other. Belbin thought that each team should include thinking roles, action roles
and people-orientated roles.

Thinking roles

* A **plant** who is creative and innovative
* A **monitor evaluator** who can make crucial decisions
* A **specialist** who is expert in a particular area.

Action roles

* A **shaper** who is single minded and inspirational
* An **implementer** who is conscientious, liking routine and tidiness
* A **completer-finisher** who is hard working and meets deadlines.

People-orientated roles

- A **coordinator** who can direct and motivate the group and organize resources
- A **resource investigator** who excels at negotiating and researching
- A **team worker** who focuses on the smooth running of the groups.

Reflection 4.8

- Think how Belbin's team roles could be linked to creative and media jobs. Would the 'plant' be successful as a set designer or scriptwriter? Would a theatre producer or newspaper editor have to be a 'monitor evaluator' or would they also need to be a 'coordinator' and a 'shaper'? Does a researcher need to have the characteristics of the 'resource investigator'? Must a floor manager be a 'team worker'?

- Do learners just ask their friends to work with them on a project rather than people with different characteristics and skills who will make a more effective team?

The team-building process

It is recognized that once formed, teams go through different stages. It may take some time for learners to get used to other people's strengths and weaknesses. To be effective a team may need to go through the following stages: forming, norming, storming and performing, first identified and developed by Tuckman.[6]

Forming stage

People need time to get to know one another's roles, goals, personalities and skills. Time should be spent in team building. The team should have a clear understanding of the proposal and treatment for the media product they are making. They should be aware of their responsibilities and those of others, for example booking equipment, writing a 300-word news article. They must fully understand the implications of various deadlines, such as the script must be written two weeks before production starts.

Norming stage

The group needs to establish working practices, rules and standards. Schedules and meetings will be organized, for example minutes of meetings will accurately record decisions. Producers, editors or directors will be encouraging all team members to contribute to the project.

Storming stage

At some point individuals will get frustrated or angry for a number of reasons such as slow progress, disagreements over ideas, or dominant individuals. There may be a lack of trust or some team members may feel they do not really belong. These issues must be brought out into the open at production meetings and resolved.

Performing stage

Now the team should be motivated and beginning to achieve their goals. The team will trust and support each other; contingency plans are put into operation to solve problems. Products and performances are produced to the required standard and to meet the deadline.

Reflection 4.9

- How might your learners use the forming, norming, storming and performing stages to review their success in working together as a team?

Project and production management

Project management is needed for the production of a single product or event such as a brochure to the staging of a large event such as a rock concert or art exhibition. Production management can be defined as the control of ongoing, everyday production or performance processes, for instance opening the doors to the public, selling tickets, showing visitors around, making health and safety checks for a permanent exhibition.

Skills required for project managers

As in any type of management, certain skills and personal qualities are needed in order to carry out different project management functions. In the creative and media industries, management skills include the following:

- *Team management*: recruiting staff with appropriate skills, motivating staff, maintaining good working relationships between team members, delegating work and allocating responsibilities appropriately, establishing clear methods of communication and work pipelines or lines of command, providing training if necessary, organizing meetings, liaising with outside organizations.
- *Financial control*: raising finance, keeping the project or running costs within the budget, checking that money is being spent where planned, making sure that all funds can be accounted for.
- *Time management*: organizing a schedule, keeping the project on schedule, planning for contingencies.
- *Resources management*: maintaining equipment in good working order, ordering sufficient supplies of consumables, allocate or supervise work areas such as studios, editing suites, computer suites, locations for filming or recording sound.
- *Quality control*: evaluating work in progress, making sure the final product is fit for purpose; ensuring product demonstrates high aesthetic and technical standards.
- *Decision-making on content*: ideas generation, inclusion of material, editorial decisions, formulating a creative strategy, such as choose a house style for a magazine.

- *Taking legal responsibility*: for health and safety by carrying out risk assessments or training staff in safety procedures, also for sector specific laws such as copyright.
- *Taking ethical responsibility*: establishing ethical boundaries, maintaining good public relations, protecting the environment.
- *Anticipating and solving a range of problems*: this applies to all of the above.

Personal qualities required for project managers

In order to carry out the functions above, a project manager should have the following personal qualities:

- *Effective communication and interpersonal skills*: these demonstrate the ability to write clear and accurate reports, speak to a range of people using a suitable tone and vocabulary, listen to other people's points of view, assess team members' strengths and weaknesses, make clear presentations.
- *Temperamental qualities*: decisive, patient, creative, confident, analytical, punctual, organized, methodical, ability to lead, good under pressure, able to justify decisions, far seeing, committed to their work, flexible, focused on goals.
- *Technical knowledge*: even if the project manager does not have the same level of practical, specialist skills of other team members such as the camera crew, the manager should still have sufficient technical knowledge to be able to communicate and be aware of new technological developments.
- *Commercial awareness*: most projects will be carried out to make a profit, and so the manager must always be aware of the competition and keep up-to-date.
- *ICT skills:* being able to word process will be expected, but competence in using other software packages such as Excel for accounting or PowerPoint for presentations will be useful.
- *Dedication*: above all a manager must be prepared to work the required hours and set a good example to other team members.

Learners can sometimes have the perception that in their teams, only one person can be a project manager but within a large art and design, media or performing arts organization or company, although a project manager may have overall responsibility for a number of these areas above they will also have support from managers in other departmental teams such as research, finance, marketing, distribution, and legal. In large organizations there will be a number of projects running simultaneously and a number of project managers (with a range of titles) operating within the organization.

Hierarchical and flexible structures

In a traditional hierarchical structure it is very clear who has to report to whom and individual responsibilities are clearly defined (see Figure 4.1).

The trend now is for a flatter more flexible structure where people work in sometimes short-lived teams, rather than departments. They may be members of two or

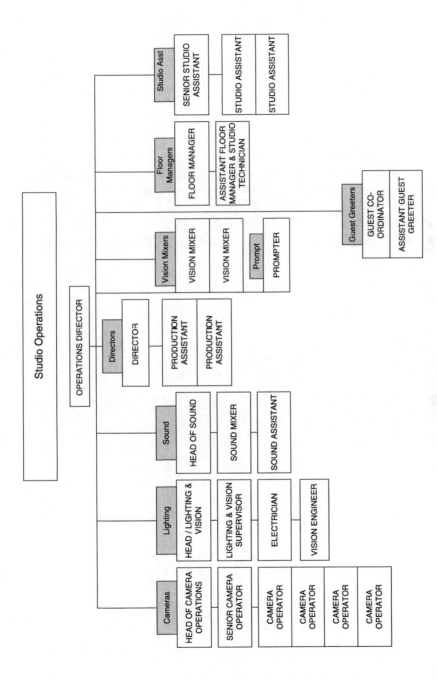

Figure 4.1 Management structure (organogram) of a typical TV studio operation

three teams working on different projects. As the workload fluctuates, people can join or leave the teams. Box 4.4 gives an example.

Box 4.4 A creative manager's workload

Asja is the creative manager for a multimedia company based in London. All employees work very closely together under the managing director and they will be working on a number of new and up and running projects at any one time. Asja does not have a typical day – that is one reason why the job is interesting. 'My contract says I work nine to five thirty but there are lots of times when I find myself working extra hours – late nights and weekends to meet a deadline.' Asja usually starts the day with catching up on emails relating to various projects that are running. Hong Kong is eight hours ahead so employees there will be well into the day's work and wanting answers. Teams on site for location projects may also need contact with her, and depending on their time zone this can occur at any hour. Every couple of days she holds a meeting with all teams to check that they understand where they are going with the brief they are working on. They discuss ideas and look at designs. Often, she contacts her clients to talk about proposals or designs either face-to-face or by making phone calls or conference calls. The rest of her day is spent programming.

Reflection 4.10

- Which of the project manager's skills and personal qualities listed above does Asja need?
- In which other creative and media areas might Asja be able to project manage?
- What opportunities do you provide for your learners to develop their management or organizational skills?

We hope that this chapter has emphasized the importance of sets of skills that underpin innovative and successful creative work. Learners who develop the skills identified in this chapter will not only be able to work with others to develop and produce creative arts and media products to gain a qualification but also improve their opportunities for employment in a wide range of industry sectors.

References

1   Young and Rubicam's 4Cs is available at www.4cs.yr.com/global [Accessed 23 April]. See also Keegan, W. and Schlegelmilch, B. (2001) *Global Marketing Management: A European Perspective*, 12th edn. Harlow: Pearson Education.
2   Experian. Available from: www.experian.co.uk/business-strategies/mosaic-uk-2009.html [Accessed 23 July 2010].
3   Wikihow. Available from: www.wikihow.com/Conduct-a-Face-to-Face-Interview-for-Journalists [Accessed 23 July 2010].

4   Webcredible.   Available   from: www.webcredible.co.uk/user-friendly-resources/web-usability/focus-groups.shtml [Accessed 23 July 2010].
5   Belbin, R. (2010) *Team Roles at Work*, 2nd edn. Oxford: Elsevier.
6   Tuckman, B. (1965) Developmental sequence in small groups, *Psychological Bulletin*, 83(6): 384–99.

Useful websites

Learning and Skills Improvement Service (LSIS) Excellence Gateway Creating Ideas resource: http://tlp.excellencegateway.org.uk/teachingandlearning/downloads/default.aspx#/creative_k247e5f93 [Accessed 23 July 2010].

Writing bibliographies: www.usingenglish.com/resources/bibliographies.html [Accessed 2 April 2010].

Citing references: the following resource includes a downloadable document on how to cite references using the Harvard (author-date) method. Bournemouth University (2010) *BU Guide to Citation in the Harvard Style*. Available from: www.bournemouth.ac.uk/library/citing-references/docs/Citing-Refs.pdf [Accessed 11 October 2010].

Young and Rubicam's Cross Cultural Consumer Characterization (4Cs). Includes online questionnaire: www.4cs.yr.com/global/ [Accessed 23 July 2010].

Belbin Associates home page: www.belbin.com [Accessed 23 July 2010].

Useful guidance on how to produce a business plan can be found at: www.bplans.co.uk/sample_business_plans.cfm [Accessed 23 July 2010].

www.businesslink.gov.uk/bdotg/action/layer?topicId=1073869162&site=210&r.s=e&r.l1=1073858805&r.lc=en&r.l3=1075215800&r.l2=1073859137&r.i=1075216102&r.t=RESOURCES [Accessed 23 July 2010].

Useful guidance on how to produce a marketing plan can be found at: www.businesslink.gov.uk/bdotg/action/layer?topicId=1073869186&site=210&r.s=e&r.l1=1073858805&r.lc=en&r.l3=1075215800&r.l2=1073859137&r.i=1075216102&r.t=RESOURCES [Accessed 23 July 2010].

Useful guidance on how to reach your customers can be found at: www.businesslink.gov.uk/bdotg/action/layer?topicId=1073918813&site=210&r.s=e&r.l1=1073858805&r.lc=en&r.l3=1075215800&r.l2=1073859137&r.i=1075216102&r.t=RESOURCES [Accessed 23 July 2010].

Useful resources related to team building can be found at: www.teamtechnology.co.uk/tt/h-articl/tb-basic.htm [Accessed 23 July 2010].

Further reading

Bell, J. (2003) *Doing your Research Project: A Guide for First-time Researchers in Education and Social Science*, 4th edn. Buckingham: Open University Press.

Cleland, D.I. and Ireland, L.R. (2006) *Project Management: Strategic Design and Implementation*, 5th edn. New York: McGraw-Hill Professional.

Cottrell, S. (2003) *The Study Skills Handbook*, 2nd edn. Basingstoke: Palgrave Macmillan.

Dolowitz, D., Buckler, S. and Sweeney, F. (2008) *Researching On Line*. Basingstoke: Palgrave Macmillan.

Emm, A. (2002) *Research for TV and Radio*. London: Routledge.

Tuckman, B. W. and Jensen, M. A. (1977) Stages of small-group development revisited. *Group Organizational Studies*, 2(4): 419–427.

5

Learning and teaching strategies

By the end of this chapter, you will be able to:

- Understand how different pedagogic approaches can support creative arts and media learners
- Recognize how the teacher as facilitator can use differentiation to support achievement
- Plan effective and interesting creative arts and media sessions and schemes of work

Introduction

This chapter explores different pedagogic approaches and their application to creative arts and media learning and discusses how teachers can use a variety of teaching and learning techniques and strategies to help learners develop their understanding. We then go on to consider how a variety of approaches through differentiated learning can support the planning of individual sessions and schemes of work.

We are privileged to be working in such rich areas of the curriculum. The creative arts and media curriculum offers an exciting and often different learning experience from that of other curriculum areas. It allows the exploration of the way ideas are generated, manipulated, presented and evaluated and the material that we can use is all around us. Learners often use their own experiences, ideas and responses to stimuli as starting points or stages in their creative journey. In doing this, they are developing their own creative processes, identifying approaches to problem solving and shaping their responses and attitudes to the world they live in.

Understanding how different pedagogic approaches can support creative arts and media learners

Creative arts and media industries and the curriculum

There is a view that the creative arts and media curriculum should be taught for its own sake and that the skills, sensitivities and attributes associated with creative and artistic endeavour should not be tainted with the needs of industry and commerce. It is true that some of our greatest artists were not thinking about how to market their work when they created it and some teachers feel that the 'industrialization' of the creative arts and media curriculum demeans and diminishes the process of discovery and wonder that is at the centre of creative thought.

However, education needs to provide the essentials for a fulfilling and productive life and the nurturing of our learner's creativity needs to be part of that preparation to be effective, productive and happy individuals. We also need to celebrate the fact that the creative and media industries are increasingly important not just within our own economy, but the world economy and it would be wrong to ignore the needs of the industries in which the UK excels. We need to support the development of creative approaches within all aspects of the curriculum, providing workers within any industry with the abilities and professional skills they need to become valuable creative contributors.

All Our Futures: Creativity, Culture and Education

Perhaps one of the most influential reports into creative teaching and learning was produced by the National Advisory Committee on creative and cultural education, published in 1999.[1] Entitled *All Our Futures: Creativity, Culture and Education,* this report set out in great detail the need for a national strategy for creativity in education.

In brief, *All Our Futures* identified the following necessary conditions to ensure the development of creativity in schools.

Learning organizations need to:

- Provide learning and teaching methods within a curriculum that allow learners space to express their own ideas, values and feelings
- Provide appropriate support to ensure that the most productive use is made of creative opportunities
- Provide not only freedom to experiment but also skills, knowledge and understanding.

Teachers need to:

- Allow for both broad and narrowly focused experimental activity
- Always specify and explain the purpose of the activity
- Help learners to feel prepared and secure enough to be willing to take risks and make mistakes

- Create non-threatening atmospheres that challenge but reassure
- Encourage an appropriate attitude towards imaginative activity, accompanied by a sense of delayed scepticism and distance
- Encourage self-expression that is oriented towards a given task
- Convey an appreciation of the phases in creative activity and the importance of time – including the ways in which time away from a problem may facilitate its solution
- Support an awareness of the differing contexts in which ideas may occur and of the roles of intuition, unconscious mental processes and non-directed thought in creative thinking
- Encourage and stimulate learners with ideas and conjecture about possibilities but complement this with critical evaluation in testing out these ideas
- Emphasize the use of imagination, originality, curiosity and questioning
- Provide an offer of choice
- Create the environment where personal attributes that facilitate creativity can be developed.

Reflection 5.1

Review the two lists above. Consider one or two of these points that you are satisfied that you do well in your teaching and ask yourself how you deliver these.

- Do you consciously plan to do this, or is it something that you feel you do instinctively?
- Now consider one or two bullet points that you feel you do not deliver so well. How could you do this better?
- What are the implications for your planning, for the learners and for your organization if you do these well?

The *All Our Futures* report also suggested that learners need to:

- Understand that creativity often develops through an iterative process that allows initial drafting or expression of ideas which are subsequently refined over time
- Develop their skills in problem solving and critical appraisal
- Know where they are in the creative process and when in that process it is appropriate to evaluate and review
- Develop a sense of excitement, respect, hope and wonder at the potential that creativity has for transformation.

Reflection 5.2

Consider the four bullet points above.

- How do we deliver a curriculum that develops skills, knowledge and a sense of excitement through an iterative learning process?
- What do you feel should be added to the list of learner needs?
- There are many pressures, both internal and external, to the organization in which we work. How can we ensure that we do not lose sight of the fundamental reasons why we deliver creative and media learning with the background of league tables, inspection, self-assessment and a welter of other issues and concerns?

Where are we now?

Since the publication of *All Our Futures* in 1999, the educational landscape has changed considerably and particularly so in creative arts and media education. Not long ago, commentators were asking why there were so many media studies learners in schools and colleges. Why were there so many graduates with degrees in media when jobs did not exist for them? What was the point in studying for media jobs when we needed learners with *real* skills? Interestingly, however, despite the changes to job roles and working patterns that the new digital technology has created, media job opportunities have been increasing over the past few years at a greater rate than many other jobs in other sectors of the economy. As part of this success story there is a recognition that the United Kingdom continues to be a world leader in the creative arts and media industries.

Some of the pedagogical approaches that were articulated within *All Our Futures* and seen as being of benefit to creative education, have now been identified as being of benefit across all of the 14+ curriculum. Having a creative approach to learning is as important as being analytical or being a problem solver. Hence the inclusion of 'creative thinker' in the personal learning and thinking skills framework.

Bloom's taxonomy and creative arts and media learning

Learners need to develop their knowledge and their intellectual skills. They need to develop their cognitive abilities to recognize and recall facts, understand intellectual processes and concepts that include the mental skills of comprehension, application, analysis, synthesis and evaluation. They also need to be able to comprehend and apply ideas before they can successfully analyse, synthesize and evaluate. You may recognize in this Bloom's cognitive learning domain theories and the hierarchical idea of development where learners build their knowledge and understanding from simple recall to the complexities of synthesis and evaluation.[2] We consider Bloom's taxonomy in relation to creative arts and media teaching in our reflections below.

The cognitive domain

The cognitive domain identified by Bloom is shown in Figure 5.1 and detailed below. Of course, Bloom's theories apply to the process of education as a whole, but one of

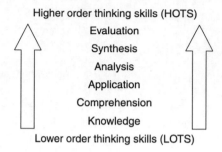

Figure 5.1 Bloom's hierarchy of thinking skills

the reasons why creative arts and media education is so exciting and rewarding to teach is that we can help the learner to develop across all of the 'domains' identified by Bloom by providing a rich, emotionally and intellectually fulfilling learning experience. The examples below begin with the lower order thinking skills and progress to higher order thinking skills in each of the domains.

Knowledge
Examples include the following:

- Listing props needed for a stage production.
- Outlining processes in creating a print product.

Comprehension
Examples include the following:

- Using own words to state a problem encountered in editing digital images.
- Interpreting meaning in a dance performance.

Application
Examples include the following:

- Using concepts such as denotation and connotation and apply to create a new book or CD cover.
- Applying learning of health and safety in a new and unfamiliar situation on work experience in a design studio.

Analysis
Examples include the following:

- Comparing and contrasting productions of *Macbeth*.
- Deconstructing a film sequence to understand the narrative process.

Synthesis

One example is as follows:

- Combining separate ideas from team members to run, plan and curate an exhibition.

Evaluation

One example is as follows:

- Considering and examining ideas in other creative and media learners' work in order to judge their value, quality, importance or extent.

Reflection 5.3

Bloom identified the above learning elements as hierarchical. The lower orders of intellectual activity being knowledge and comprehension based and the higher order thinking skills as being synthesis and evaluation. It is useful to consider the developmental journey for learners from the acquisition of facts and information to the more sophisticated processes involved with analysis, synthesis and evaluation.

- If you teach entry level or level 1 learners, is it possible to develop the skills of synthesis and evaluation at these levels when working in the creative arts and media curriculum?

The affective and psychomotor domains

Bloom identified two other 'domains', the affective and psychomotor domains. These domains are also hierarchical, with the lower orders of the affective domain relating to receiving and responding to ideas or stimuli and the higher order skills being able to organize and internalize.

Good creative arts and media teaching develops learners emotionally as well as intellectually and can, of course, help to develop their psychomotor skills. One of the strengths of our area is that we can help learners to develop confidence and a positive attitude to their work. This may be more apparent in some areas of the creative arts and media curriculum than in others. However, we can increase all learners' skill levels in the affective and psychomotor domains by the careful planning of our learning sessions and in the way in which we assess learning. The study of dance, acting, music making and composition are all areas of creative arts and media education that are as easy to identify as those that help develop these skills and attributes in learners.

In the psychomotor domain, perception and set are identified as lower order skills and adaptation and origination being the highest order. As with the cognitive domain model, the affective and psychomotor domains are as well served through the medium of creative arts and media learning as the development of intellectual skills. Learners' feelings, their enthusiasm, motivation, attitudes, perceptions and values and their ability to perceive and understand nuance, the communication of meaning through complex patterns of movement or dexterity can all be developed through creative arts and media learning.

The development of physical movement, coordination, and use of the motor-skill areas requires learners to experience an iterative process and through practice, the learner has the opportunity to improve. Psychomotor skills are measured in terms of speed, precision and the development of techniques in the execution of the skill.

Affective domain

Receive
Examples include the following:

- Listening sensitively to other people's ideas about your work.
- Tolerating other people's opinions about the value of work in an art gallery.

Respond
Examples include the following:

- Actively participating in production meetings.
- Reacting to client feedback to improve a product.

Value
Examples include the following:

- Recognizing the value of other people's contributions in your drama team.
- Being able to internalize and commit to a set of values and expressing these values when writing news stories.

Organize
Examples include the following:

- Organizing priorities and values when creating advertising copy.
- Resolving conflicts between team members when directing a film crew.

Internalize
Examples include the following:

- Becoming self-reliant in organizing and carrying out production work.
- Revising judgement of performance in the light of the director's comments.

Psychomotor domain

Perception
Examples include the following:

- Responding to cues from the director of a play and moving upstage.
- Following the conductor and orchestral lead to play a piece of music.

Set
One example is as follows:

- Using mental, physical and emotional mindsets to perform well in an audition.

Guided response
One example is as follows:

- Learning how to operate the mixing desk through trial and error and practice.

Mechanism
One example is as follows:

- Developing dance steps so that they become habitual and can be performed with increasing confidence and proficiency.

Complex overt response
One example is as follows:

- Skilfully performing complex hand drawing techniques with increasing proficiency and skill, characterized by accuracy, coordination and efficiency. Performance is automatic and without hesitation.

Adaptation
One example is as follows:

- Modifying piano style to fit requirements for different keyboards and performance areas such as a concert hall or restaurant.

Origination
One example is as follows:

- Creating vocal extemporizations or instrumental riffs for a new cover version of a song demonstrating highly developed skills creatively used.

Reflection 5.4

- Review the affective and psychomotor domains. Identify a level within each domain where your learners generally perform well. How could you organize and plan your teaching to move your learners up to the next level?
- Who can support you in analysing your teaching and evaluating the opportunities that are open to you to develop these aspects of learning?

Creative arts and media education helps learners to develop across the cognitive, affective and psychomotor domains, and by reflecting on our practice, it is always possible to find new ways to teach and provide a more diverse experience for our learners and in the process create more challenge and insight for ourselves. By articulating what we do, we can analyse and better understand our practice.

Where are we now? Higher order thinking skills

Bloom's taxonomies were a product of the 1950s, a time before the Internet, a time when teachers were educating for an industrial economy. If commentators were questioning the need for media studies graduates in the first decade of the twenty-first century, there was very little recognition that a creative education (although Bloom recognized creativity as part of the synthesizing process) was a necessity for the majority of learners in the middle of the twentieth century. Today, as we have argued in this book, much educational thinking is concentrated on the creative aspects of learning.

Lorin Anderson, a former student of Bloom, has revisited Bloom's taxonomy and made some interesting and fundamental changes to the model.[3] He changed the nouns into verbs, making the process immediately appear much more dynamic (Figure 5.2). Anderson renamed and changed the order of some of the different aspects in the model, interestingly changing 'synthesis' to 'creating'. This new taxonomy reflects a more active form of thinking and perhaps more accurately describes an emphasis on an active approach to learning.

Other educationalists such as Michael Pohl[4] and Andrew Churches[5] identify how this new model is particularly applicable to the ways in which we learn, manage and manipulate information and knowledge in the Internet age.

It does seem to make sense that creating in its widest sense is of the highest order as all of the other learning and thinking skills in the hierarchy come into play. The 'doing' words point up the dynamic nature of creative education and the higher order thinking skills (HOTS) of creating, evaluating and analysing. These are the skills that we want our learners to be continually applying in a range of different problem-solving contexts.

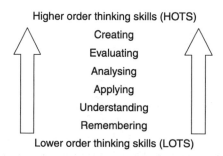

Higher order thinking skills (HOTS)

Creating

Evaluating

Analysing

Applying

Understanding

Remembering

Lower order thinking skills (LOTS)

Figure 5.2 Lorin Anderson's updated version of Bloom's hierarchy of thinking skills

> **Reflection 5.5**
>
> Think about a particular group of your learners. They do not need to be studying at a high level and in many ways this activity challenges us as teachers more when we consider younger learners or those with lower ability. How do we plan activities in which our learners can develop these HOT skills? You may prefer to consider Bloom's original cognitive taxonomy or the new interpretation by Lorin Anderson (Figures 5.1 and 5.2).

Recognizing how the teacher as facilitator can use differentiation to support achievement

By structuring learning, we provide routes that a range of learners with different learning preferences need to follow in order to absorb and manipulate information and develop their own ideas. Learning can be broken down into different activities that support different learner preferences. In these activities, the teacher is a facilitator rather than a didactic deliverer of knowledge. Facilitation does not imply non-engagement or a lesser role for the teacher.

For example, a teacher may wish to introduce a new idea to learners, such as Edward Gordon Craig's ideas on stage design. The learners may be asked to carry out research, or the teacher may provide information that learners need to retain in order to develop further their own ideas in a later session.

To ensure that learners have understood this introduction to Craig's work, the teacher may ask them to:

- Complete a quiz or a test.
- Work in teams to *describe* Craig's use of light.
- *Identify* his ideas in relation to action, words, line, colour and rhythm.
- *Label* or *list* or *reproduce* elements of his work so that they can *recall* his ideas and *define* important elements in his theories.

In other words, the teacher is developing and expanding the learners' knowledge base through *selecting information* and *remembering*. They are at the first stage of understanding Craig's ideas of theatre design. To develop their understanding, the teacher might ask the learners to:

- *Compare* Craig's ideas with, for instance, one of Brecht's collaborators, Caspar Neher, who they may have studied earlier in their programme of learning and to *summarize* the differences in approach.
- *Interpret* the reasons for the different application of the ideas. This will move their understanding on so that they are able to *apply* their understanding through *creating* a design of their own by *executing* and *implementing* Craig's ideas.
- *Analyse* the constituent parts of Craig's theories by *deconstructing* the elements of his ideas and *evaluating* their effectiveness.

- Consider whether his ideas have any resonance for them and *examine* them in order to *judge* their value, quality, importance or the extent in which they have been influential.
- *Create* their own work by *assembling* or *reorganizing elements* of Craig's ideas in an assignment that asks them to produce a stage design based on his original ideas but *generating new patterns, structures and ideas* of their own.

Reflection 5.6

- How can the teacher facilitate the learning processes identified above?
- How can teachers facilitate learners in extending their thinking and learning through questioning their own and others' assumptions, being flexible enough to adapt ideas and plans when circumstances change, trying out these alternatives and being able to carry out tasks to their planned or refocused conclusions?

Facilitation is not about letting learners sink or swim, it is about an investment in planning time and the provision of an environment in which learners feel supported but can develop their ideas and recognize the ways in which they learn. By structuring and facilitating learning in this way, we are supporting learners to become 'expert learners', enabling them to work in partnership with their teachers so that they are not merely consumers of education, but are active participators who are empowered to create their own learning opportunities, be resilient in the face of problems and know how to succeed.

Building differentiation into learning

Creative arts and media education is a rich learning environment; however, we do need to consciously build differentiated learning opportunities into the curriculum that we offer to our learners. A differentiated approach treats learners as individuals.

At its most basic, when planning sessions a teacher may identify differentiated outcomes that provide opportunities for individuals to do the following:

- Carry out different tasks that meet individual interests and needs, such as when producing a newspaper, learners with good drawing skills produce a cartoon script, while those who enjoy writing produce feature articles.
- Include tasks that stretch and challenge, for instance asking a learner to act as film director.
- Produce evidence in formats that play to their strengths, such as a verbal presentation rather than a written report.
- Have extra support, for example one-to-one support from a teaching assistant, specialist equipment to produce text.

But at a deeper level, we need to consider how differentiation helps individual learners develop the skills, knowledge and attributes to be effective learners, citizens and workers. We need to consider how, through a variety of approaches, we are able to support individual learners to articulate and internalize what we are teaching. We cannot just assume that learners will absorb what we teach. We need to identify, within our session planning, where these learning opportunities exist and overtly provide learners with a framework within which they can recognize their strengths and areas in which to improve.

Planning effective and interesting creative arts and media sessions and schemes of work

A scheme of work should take into account the whole learner journey including initial advice and guidance, induction, opportunities for applied learning and work experience, assessment points (see Chapter 7) and progression.

Careers education information, advice and guidance, recruitment, induction and initial assessment

If the learner is not on the right programme, one that motivates them and allows them to progress, reach their potential and support them in achieving their aspirations, they are more likely to drop out or not achieve their potential. The work of the teacher will also be far more difficult and less rewarding. To help learners make the appropriate decision about their programme of study, they need effective careers education, information, advice and guidance (CEIAG), and an induction period that includes initial assessments and an introduction to the way they will be expected to learn.

Careers education, information, advice and guidance will do the following:

- Provide information related to the key features above in terms that the learner can understand
- Provide publicity and information that is accurate and up-to-date
- Check that learners' expectations (e.g. to do voluntary work as an assistant stage manager in local theatre or do a degree in film after the course) are realistic and can be met through the programme
- Provide guidance on alternative options
- Inform learners about progression routes.

To be effective, induction for full-time courses should be extended to more than a couple of days before a course starts. For learners on programmes on shorter courses or different modes of study, an induction is equally important. Induction will provide learners with the opportunity to

- Sample the type of work they will carry out during the programme
- Get to know the staff and the educational institution
- Understand the ethos and rules of the institution and programme
- Familiarize themselves with the features of their programme

- Bond with their peers
- Gain access to specialist advice and support
- Undergo initial assessments for English, mathematics and ICT
- Be empowered to ask questions about their learning programme and ask for help.

Initial assessment in English is particularly necessary for creative arts and media learners and a significant number of learners may be dyslexic. To be successful in the creative industries, they will need effective communication skills. Many roles, for example a journalist, advertising copywriter or designer, will require a high standard of speaking, listening, reading and writing. Other roles will require proficiency in using ICT and mathematics. (For more information on functional skills, see Chapter 3.)

Applied learning

Helping learners to understand the application of their learning to the sector that they are studying is good practice in any learning programme. What we mean by applied learning is the opportunity for learners to engage in learning activities that help them to understand how their learning relates to the real world. Creative arts and media learning is not something that exists within a cocoon within the school or college. Applied learning reaches out and draws on the experience and inspiration of practitioners working in a range of creative and media industries. It helps to make sense of learning and validates the learners' experiences and findings. It supports their preparation for the world of work or higher-level study.

This approach to learning is appropriate for a range of teaching and learning within the creative art and media curriculum. When learners understand that their learning has an application in the real world, it makes sense to them and supports their motivation and engagement. Interesting and effective teaching sessions can be generated through a wide range of stimuli. Here are just a few of them:

- Partnership with local practitioners, for example:
    - local artists and creative practitioners
    - theatre companies, dance companies
    - design studios
    - finding the creative partnership opportunities in existing links with the world of work
    - local radio and television
    - local media companies.

- Working with local employers who may have creative design or media functions.
- Work shadowing and presenting back to the class 'A day in the life of . . .'.
- Working with large employers such as local authorities or hospitals. How are they creative environments? What creative activities take place? Who is available to talk to?

- Visiting museums, libraries, large public open spaces. What are they used for? Who arranges 'Proms in the Park' or the open-air pop concert? How are the summer entertainment activities planned and performed?
- Supporting non-creative and media organizations to produce publicity, market or promote their products or services.
- Working with voluntary organizations (the Third Sector) to help them to communicate their message or fund raise. Supporting charitable activities and social enterprise. Understanding how these organizations rely on the expertise inherent in creative and media activity and individuals.
- Participating in events, festivals and so on.
- Using expertise that exists within the school or college – part-time or sessional staff who also have other (portfolio) careers in the arts.

Work experience

Creative arts and media learners can benefit greatly from experiencing the 'real world' of work. Being able to observe and talk to a range of practitioners such as researchers and technicians as well as managers, editors and directors are valuable experiences for learners to understand how their learning relates to professional practice. If they are appropriately prepared with the skills including social skills and the personal attributes, particularly energy and enthusiasm, that enable them to participate with activities in the workplace, they have a great deal to offer to potential employers. They can provide increased capacity at times when creative and media organizations have a tight print or project deadline to meet or are about to present a show. To get the best out of the experience, there needs to be careful planning, a consideration of learners' expectations and an understanding of what they can bring to the situation.

Learning can also be brought to life by using creative and media practitioners to do the following:

- Working with the teacher to produce real industry briefs or briefs that have realistic expectations regarding timescales, budget and design constraints.
- Writing assignments, bringing a real work flavour to practical and theoretical aspects of learning.
- Participating in the assessment of work and provide feedback on products and performances.
- Making visits to the classroom to present their ideas, their ways of working and industry norms.
- Giving appropriate feedback on the feasibility of learners' ideas and supporting learners' research.

Helping learners to appreciate the real world of creative practitioners can have surprising results (see Box 5.1).

Box 5.1 A sculptor in the real world

Sandra, a school teacher, brought in a sculptor, Jamie, to talk about how to be awarded a commission for his work. The learners were amazed to discover that Jamie had to consider such issues as health and safety legislation when bidding for a commission. He needed to be able to respond to questions about how his sculpture may present hazards, relate to traffic flows (location on a traffic island) and be a potential target for vandalism. In presenting ideas to commissioning organizations such as local authorities, Jamie had to rework his designs so that his sculptures could not be climbed on, or jumped off. He had to make compromises regarding the artistic vision of his work because of prosaic considerations. All of this was in addition to his creative work in his studio. Learners understood, very clearly, how generic and transferable skills were crucial to him in securing the commission.

When visits or work experiences take place, there needs to be proper and effective risk assessment that includes assessing health and safety risks as well as safeguarding all learners. There are different statutory requirements depending on the age of the learners and it is important to consider that there may be some activities that would be unsuitable for younger or vulnerable learners.

Residentials and summer schools are ideal ways in which teachers and professional practitioners can support learners in a controlled and safe environment. Some creative arts and media courses start with residential activities with professional input towards the end of the summer term, before they start in earnest in the autumn.

Session planning

Although we have focused on active and facilitated learning, this is not a replacement for other learning methods. Sometimes learners need to be gathered together and taught something in a more didactic way. Sometimes they need to be told things, they certainly need explanations and they need to know how they are achieving by having regular timely and supportive feedback. The inclusion of applied learning supports the differentiated needs of our learners and makes our lives as teachers as interesting and rewarding as the learners' lives. Creative and media teachers need to have a range of tools available to be able to respond to a wide range of learning situations in an appropriate way. Deciding which tools to use can be identified in the session plan.

The format for session plans are individual to the organization in which you work. However, there should be some common elements.

- Session aims and objectives (to be shared with learners).
- Recap on previous session, introduction or sharing session objectives (limited to three or four).
- Learners' prior knowledge and skills required: how the session follows on from previous learning.
- Lesson type, for instance practical, theory, tutorial (group or individual).

- Every child, learner or person matters issues.
- Use of technology.
- How the session promotes equality and diversity. Consider incipient sexism, other prejudice etc.
- Timescale and structure, for example:
  - warmup activity
  - main body of learning
  - opportunities for assessment and feedback – teacher, self, peer, group
  - plenary – recap and reflection on session and what was learnt.
- How you differentiate the learning outcomes and activities for your range of learners.
- How you develop extension activities.
- Opportunities to diagnose, develop and assess functional skills and PLTS.
- Assessment and feedback opportunities.
- Range of activities and teaching strategies to be used.
- Interactions:
  - learner–learner
  - learner–teacher
  - learners–professional practitioners etc.
- Ways of working: group, paired work.
- Space – for learners to reflect and think.
- Opportunity for self-evaluation (by you, of the session).
- Opportunity for learner evaluation (of the session).
- Homework and/or preparation for next session.
- Health and safety, risk assessments and safeguarding issues.
- Resources.

Reflection 5.7

Consider the six examples below of activities that might develop creativity. Reflect on when they might be used within a session (e.g. as an icebreaker), as a main activity, or to work in pairs and groups.

1 The following activity can quickly generate ideas for a story, film, play, dance or picture. Tell individual learners to draw their favourite animal in the middle of a sheet of paper. (Skills in drawing are not needed!) Ask them to draw another animal they like by the side of the big animal. Ask them to draw an animal they do not like in the corner. Then ask them to list adjectives describing the animal's character underneath the images. You might also ask them to indicate a colour associated with each animal. Tell the learners that the main animal represents their chief character in their story, dance etc. The smaller animal is the 'sidekick'

or friend of the main character. The animal they do not like represents the villain. The activity can then be extended so that learners think about how the relationship between the three is likely to develop.

2   Ask learners to create a quiz relating to a work of art, media product or performance and the processes involved in creating it to use with peers.

3   Ask learners to individually draw two frames of a storyboard. Then ask them to work in small groups to create one storyboard that uses at least one element from each learners' individual frames. The elements could be the characters, the style of drawing, and the storyline.

4   The basic concept behind this activity is stereotyping. Show learners a picture of a landscape from a newspaper or magazine or a work of art with which they are unfamiliar. Ask them to write on a piece of paper why they think this is a good place to visit and when they think the photograph or artwork was produced. Ask learners to compare their 'assumption' with others and question alternative assumptions.

5   Tell learners that they need to liaise with a client who works 30 miles away to show their work. They must work out ways to do this, e.g. video conference, travel to the client or email, and list the pros and cons of each method, e.g. cheapest or most persuasive.

6   Ask learners to estimate costings for a new fashion garment that will retail at £50. Then tell them that the client wants to retail the garment at £20. Ask them to suggest how this will affect the manufacturing process or the quality of the final garment.

Remember, session planning is for *you*, to help you to organize learning. It may be useful for cover purposes if you are absent, but its primary purpose is to help you plan. It is a discipline that helps you structure your thoughts and your reasons for the learning activities you offer your learners.

By following some of the ideas in this chapter, we hope that you are able to develop a range of learning approaches and by doing this discover new ways of learning for yourself and your learners. Developing a more facilitative role allows an element of risk into the teaching and learning relationship and that in turn helps learners to take more responsibility for their learning, develop an understanding of how they like to learn, what they need to do to improve and to try out ways of learning that they may not naturally follow. We may be the pedagogical experts, but the learners are the experts on themselves.

References

1   National Advisory Committee on Creative and Cultural Education (1999) *All Our Futures: Creativity, Culture and Education*. Available from: www.cypni.org.uk/downloads/alloutfutures.pdf [Accessed 23 July 2010].

2   Bloom, B. (1969) *Taxonomy of Educational Objectives: The Classification of Educational Goals*. London: Longman.

3   Anderson, L. and Krathwohl, D. (eds) (2000) *A Taxonomy for Learning, Teaching, and Assessing: A Revision of Bloom's Taxonomy of Educational Objectives*. Columbus, OH: Allyn & Baker.

4   Pohl, M. (2000) *Learning to Think, Thinking to Learn: Models and Strategies to Develop a Classroom Culture of Thinking.* Cheltenham, Victoria, Australia: Hawker Brownlow Education.

5   Andrew Churches. Available from: http://edorigami.wikispaces.com/Bloom%27s+and+ICT+tools [Accessed on 23 July 2010].

Useful websites

Bloom's Taxonomy Blooms Digitally. Available from: http://edweb.sdsu.edu/courses/EDTEC470/sp09/5/bloomstaxanomy.html [Accessed 23 July 2010].

Information on IAG. Available from: www.igengroup.co.uk/IAG_Consultancy [Accessed 23 July 2010].

Further reading

Boud, D. and Miller, N. (eds) (1996) *Working with Experience: Animating Learning.* London: Routledge.

Bruner, J. (1996) *Towards a Theory of Instruction.* Cambridge, MA: Harvard University Press.

Bryson, J. (1998) *Effective Classroom Management.* London: Hodder & Stoughton.

Entwhistle, N. (1988) *Styles of Learning and Teaching.* London: David Fulton.

Harkin, J. (2006) *Excellence in Supporting Applied Learning.* London: Lifelong Learning UK (LLUK).

Kolb, D.A. (1984) *Experiential Learning.* Englewood Cliffs, NJ: Prentice Hall.

Petty, G. (2004) *Teaching Today: A Practical Guide.* London: Stanley Thorne.

6
Resources

By the end of this chapter, you will be able to:

- Understand the range of resources which enable learners to understand the creative and media industries and mirror working practices
- Recognize that learning can take place outside the classroom through links and partnerships with creative and media professionals
- Plan your own continuing professional development to improve your subject knowledge and increase your impact on learning

Introduction

It is easy to focus on facilities and equipment when planning your course, especially when learners are on a practical or vocational programme, but there are other things that may be equally or even more important to consider. In this chapter we look at the different types of resources that support effective delivery and meet the needs of individual as well as groups of learners. Such resources include more traditional forms such as books and master classes as well as the latest state of the art facilities, equipment and software. We discuss how to fund resources and what makes the learning environment safe.

There is a section on resources outside the classroom and how partnerships with individuals and organizations can enhance the delivery of theoretical concepts as well as provide opportunities for practical work. There are suggestions on how to make and develop effective links.

Human resources are key for learner success. The creative and media industries need people who are effective team workers, and teachers need to model team working skills by involving their own colleagues and external creative practitioners in delivery.

As noted in Chapter 1, you may forget your own creativity in planning, delivering and assessing learner work. The final section looks at how you can maintain and develop your dual professionalism as an expert in your subject area and as an expert in teaching.

Resources which enable learners to understand the creative arts and media industries and mirror working practices

Types of resources

Whatever creative arts and media programme your learners are on, they will need to find, reinforce or develop knowledge and understanding of the products, performances, working practices or industries that they have been introduced to in your sessions.

The library

You should make sure learners are able to access a library (for example a college library or a public library) and know about the full range of library services and learning resources, such as information searches, requests for materials, loans of films. Libraries these days provide much more than just storage for books. If learners are aware of what services are offered at the start of their course and are actively encouraged to use them, they will improve the quality of their work and possibly save money on buying magazines or DVDs (digital video discs) which they can borrow.

An introduction to the library makes a valuable induction activity. It is also useful at this time to make sure that all learners understand about copyright and how to avoid accusations of plagiarism. (See the section in Chapter 4, pp. 73–5, on writing a bibliography or compiling references.)

When might you use different types of paper-based and online resources?

Books

In this age of the Internet, some creative arts and media learners can ignore books. However, because of the quality processes that study books go through (the commissioning of expert writers, editorial direction, proofreading) the content is usually accurate and aimed at a particular readership. Yes, some information may go out of date but general principles on work processes and skills will remain the same.

Subject-specific books on the performing arts, art and design or media can help both you the teacher and your learners. Such books may focus on theoretical knowledge or on practical processes. They might provide a general background or broad overview to an area like the performing arts or they might offer a more in-depth specialist view of a specific area such as pop art. They can reinforce and extend areas of knowledge or practice that you have introduced in your sessions or they may form the basis for individual learner research. Books are useful as a reference tool on your shelf or for extended reading to gain a general background to a subject.

Some textbooks are commissioned by awarding bodies and written specifically for creative arts and media qualifications. Teachers often find that it is useful to buy multiple copies of these or ask each learner to purchase their own copy. These books are valuable for supporting both teachers and learners in gaining the background knowledge needed to achieve the qualification but can result in learners just referring to one book, which can limit their wider understanding of the creative and media world.

It is particularly encouraging for learners if they are given a short list of potentially useful books at the start of their programme. However, you or a librarian should check that the language level and the content level in your reading list are appropriate for your cohort of learners. If you recommend suitable texts, make sure you inform library staff in both your organization's library and in local public libraries so that they can order sufficient copies to satisfy potential demand.

Reflection 6.1

- Think about creative and media books you found useful as a learner and teacher. Which were the most useful for you? Was it the style of writing? The use of illustrations? The detail in the content?
- Plan how you might work with colleagues and a librarian to compile an-up-to-date booklist that will be similarly useful for your learners.

Newspapers and magazines

Newspapers and magazines are particularly useful in keeping you and your learners up-to-date, for example the *Guardian*'s Monday media supplement. Your library should also contain specialist magazines. Although you cannot expect your learners to read newspapers thoroughly on a regular basis without encouragement, you can introduce activities that support them in recognizing their importance as sources of information on the creative industries.

Reflection 6.2

Look at the tasks involving newspapers and magazines listed in Table 6.1. What type of similar short activities could you develop to use with learners?

Websites

There are many websites that provide materials to support delivery. Some are aimed specifically at teachers, others at people within the industry but have sections for teachers and learners. Some are commercial, while others are free. These materials include downloadable, information sheets, lesson plans as well as interactive games and quizzes for learners. Besides materials they often offer discussion boards or blogs so that you can ask questions or share ideas with colleagues or practitioners external to your organization.

Some websites are not subject specific but occasionally contain relevant materials for teachers and learners, for example Teachers TV www.teachers.tv/ [Accessed 2 April 2010] or Connexions Direct Available from www.connexions-direct.com/

Table 6.1 Tasks involving newspapers and magazines

Focus	Task
Is it legal? Researching legal concepts	Bring a range of recent tabloid and broadsheet newspapers into the classroom. Challenge learners to work in teams to scan the newspapers for stories or articles about legal issues connected with creative and media celebrities or companies. Examples might include arguments over copyright, contracts or takeovers. The winning pair will be the learners who find the most stories
Spotting the trend! Using information on what's out there in the market to influence creative arts and media projects	Ask learners to bring in any magazines they have at home from the last month. Warn them they and their peers will be cutting up these magazines. These can be any lifestyle magazines (e.g. *HELLO!*) or specialist magazine (e.g. car magazine). Supermarket magazines are particularly good for this as they are free. Tell learners to work in a group to skim through the magazine pictures, titles and captions and note down: • Recurring colours, e.g. pink, stripes • Recurring styles, e.g. 1950s • Recurring themes, e.g. organic, global. When they have reached a consensus on what current trends are, they should cut out examples from the magazines showing these and create a mood board. They should then present their mood board to the other groups and explain how they will respond to this trend in their next project

[Accessed 2 April 2010]. Other websites contain extensive creative and media teaching and learning resources.

The LSIS Excellence Gateway Creative and Media resource contains both CPD and learner resources for creative arts and media. There are themes related to engagement with industry, planning projects, listening to learners and assessment. This is a useful resource for all creative and media areas and focuses on how ideas can be developed and pitched.

LSIS Excellence Gateway Teaching and Learning: *Creative and Media*. Available from: http://tlp.excellencegateway.org.uk/tlp/cam/resource/html/resources.php [Accessed 2 April 2010].

LSIS Excellence Gateway Teaching and Learning: *Creating Ideas*. Available from: http://tlp.excellencegateway.org.uk/teachingandlearning/downloads/default.aspx#/creative_k247e5f93 [Accessed 2 April 2010].

The LSIS Excellence Gateway also has a music resource whose themes focus on music and enterprise, intrapersonal skills, creative thinking and using digital technology.

LSIS Excellence Gateway Teaching and Learning: *Music*. Available from: http://tlp.excellencegateway.org.uk/tlp/cam/music/index.php [Accessed 2 April 2010].

If you want to keep up-to-date with developments in the creative and media industries and employment you should access the sector skills websites (see Chapter 1).

The Creative Choices website is excellent for information about careers and working practices in the creative industries with lots of case studies, podcasts and video clips.

Creative Choices. Available from: www.creative-choices.co.uk/ [Accessed 2 April 2010].

Some organizations such as theatres, agencies, archives, museums and regulatory bodies also have sections aimed at teachers and learners. For example:

National Media Museum Homepage. Available from: www.nationalmedia museum.org.uk/Home.asp [Accessed 2 April 2010].

Tate Homepage. Available from: www.tate.org.uk/ [Accessed 2 April 2010].

Flickr Homepage. Available from: www.flickr.com/tour/ [Accessed 2 April 2010].

Footage Vault Moments that Matter: *Clips for Schools*. Available from: www.foot agevault.com/schools [Accessed 2 April 2010].

BBC Archive. Available from: www.bbc.co.uk/archive/ [Accessed 2 April 2010].

Royal Academy of Music Homepage. Available from: www.ram.ac.uk/Pages/ default.aspx [Accessed 2 April 2010].

BBFC Education. Available from: www.bbfc.co.uk/education/ [Accessed 2 April 2010].

Royal Shakespeare Company Education. Available from: www.rsc.org.uk/ learning/Learning.aspx [Accessed 2 April 2010].

Reflection 6.3

Explore the websites above and find three examples of materials that might be useful to you in planning or delivering creative arts and media sessions in the near future. Think about how you might adapt some resources for different types of learners. Also think about what other organizations connected with your subject area (e.g. drama, sculpture) might have websites that can offer information or support.

Higher grades can be linked to the breadth and depth of research and how it is carried out and presented. Referencing research materials appropriately and creating bibliographies are clear ways for learners to show that their research is well organized. They should also realize that not only books but also other materials including films, websites and even blogs should be properly referenced (see Chapter 4, pp. 73–5).

Equipment, materials and software

Creative arts and media courses can require a wider range of resources than any other subject. Arts students may require not only materials such as paints, clay, textiles and canvasses but also photographic and printing equipment, computer graphic packages and exhibition stands. If they are producing installation or performance art and publicity for their work, they may also wish to access materials, equipment and software used by performing arts and media students.

You are likely to have already some equipment and materials to use with learners that may vary from drawing paper and pencils to a sophisticated digital sound and lighting desk. There are a number of factors to consider when deciding on what further resources you need. You should first carry out an audit of equipment, materials and software to find out the following:

- What resources are available
- Which learning programmes have access to them
- Whether their quantity is sufficient for access by individual or groups of learners
- If they are sufficiently up-to-date or in good condition
- Whether they can enable learners to follow current industry working practices
- How they can enhance learners' creativity
- The extent to which they enable learners to produce good quality work
- Whether they can enable learners to produce evidence to meet the needs of a qualification
- Which staff can use them and who might need training
- What level of technical support is available to maintain them
- If the resources meet the expectations of your learners.

You will never be given enough money to buy everything you want. You will always have to balance quantity against quality (e.g. two high-end PCs against ten cheap laptops) and should prioritize what features are needed. You will also need to consider whether the top of the range items will be obsolete in a few years' time. There has to be a balance between buying equipment and software used by professionals in the creative and media industries (such as Apple Macs) or buying equipment that can be used by a wider group of learners such as flipcams. (Some creative arts and media teachers find that these small and easy to use. Flipcams are great for recording learner activities as an alternative to or to support work diaries, feedback and assessment.)

All creative arts and media learners (and teachers) should have good access to items such as computers and the Internet or they can be disadvantaged. If learners cannot use up-to-date software packages to create, develop, edit and promote their work, their creativity will be limited and they will not be prepared for employment within the creative industries. This may also need access to social networking sites where they can upload their work and gain feedback under supervision. Safeguarding measures must be in place to protect not only learner work but the learners' themselves. Most schools now have intranets, learning platforms or virtual learning environments (VLEs) which can be useful for sharing information, storing assignments and learner work (see pp. 108–9).

You will need to find out who in your organization is responsible for purchasing more equipment, materials or software. When negotiating a budget for new resources you should be able to explain to a line manager the impact on learning of the new equipment and the ease of use by a number of staff, not only you.

Learners can be expected to hire or buy some resources, such as musical instruments themselves, but others, your organization will provide. Some manufacturers may also donate equipment or offer special reductions to educational organizations. If you are responsible for purchasing equipment, materials or software, it is worth shopping around. If you are buying an expensive and complex item of equipment, you should take into account whether training in its use is provided free of charge or whether you will have to pay more money for a specialist course.

Facilities

Facilities for learners include classrooms, studios (e.g. dance, photographic, art, film editing, music studios), libraries and computer suites. Unless you are very influential or lucky to be involved in the design of a new building you will have to work with the facilities that already exist. However, you are likely to be able to make some changes and decide on if, how and when you might use certain spaces.

A facility will have a positive impact on creative and media learners if

- It encourages creativity
- It enables skills to be learned, practised and developed
- It allows industry working practices to be modelled.

As noted in Chapter 1, creativity can seem to be chaotic. The traditional classroom with desks or tables and chairs arranged in rows or around the room facing a whiteboard is for most people not a creative environment.

Reflection 6.4

Think about periods when you have been most creative, for example writing a short story, practising singing, working on a dance sequence, or designing a fashion garment. Answer the questions below and then pick out three key elements that enable you to be creative and develop creative skills.

- How were you seated?
- Did you have 'ownership' of this area or did it belong to someone else?
- Did you have access to food or drink?
- Were other people in your immediate area?
- Were you at a desk?
- Did you have access to a computer?
- Did you have easy access to materials or equipment?
- Did you have space to spread around your materials and equipment?
- Did you have a pleasant view?
- Were you in a quiet area or did you have the radio on?
- Were you listening to music?
- Could you get up and walk around?
- Could you use the telephone to ask for information or advice from other people?

- Were you wearing a smart outfit and shoes, jeans and trainers, or pyjamas and slippers?
- Were you most creative in the early morning or the evening?

You may not be able to introduce some of these elements into your learners' work areas such as wearing pyjamas and slippers. However, there are other elements that might be introduced. For example, could you arrange furniture so that learners can get up and walk around? Can they have a drink at hand? Can they use their telephones to communicate with others? Can they take ownership of the area by putting up posters or examples of work?

Some teachers may have concerns that by allowing such freedoms in the learning environment, the result will be chaos. When learners are motivated and interested *in* their learning, they take more responsibility *for* their learning. The use of appropriate resources supports them in becoming expert learners. Ground rules established by the teacher and the group are needed which take into consideration the needs of others working alongside them and the ethos of the environment in which they are working.

Whenever possible the environment should mirror professional processes and practices, with the main differences being that learners can

- make mistakes
- experiment
- practise skills
- access support.

What each learner can expect when working in any creative arts and media area is to be safe. Learners should model industry practices closely.

Induction activities should ensure that they understand the implications of health and safety legislation, be able to recognize hazards and the level of risks in their work area and deal with these appropriately. Safety is not just about physical health but also about mental well-being. The creative industries are very competitive and pressurised; learning to cope with stress is useful for learners – and teachers.

Learners should regularly carry out risk assessments as part of projects and be observed following safe working practices by staff (see Table 6.2).

A useful resource that contains sections which contextualize health and safety for creative arts and media can be found on the LSIS Excellence Gateway Teaching and Learning Programme, *Health, Safety and Well-being*. Available from http://tlp.excellencegateway.org.uk/tlp/xcurricula/hswb/ [Accessed 2 April 2010].

If your facilities are not adequate, you should consider working in partnership with other external organizations such as local theatres, commercial recording studios or facilities in other schools, colleges or universities or training organizations, though these will probably charge for access (see the section on pp. 109–11 on Links and partnerships).

Table 6.2 Simple risk assessment

A simple risk assessment asks the questions	Exemplar responses
What is the hazard?	A costume left on the floor of the changing room
What is the risk?	Tripping which could result in broken bones
Who is at risk?	Dancers and actors, wardrobe staff
What is the level of risk to them?	High: they will be in a hurry to change between scenes and may not notice what is left on the floor.
How can the risk be removed or decreased?	Place all costumes on a hanger and hang on a rail as soon as they are taken off

Virtual learning environments and the Internet

In recent years intranets and VLEs have increased the use of computers and the Internet for planning, delivery and assessment.

> A virtual learning environment (VLE) is a standardised, computer-based environment that supports the delivery of web-based learning and facilitates online interaction between students and teachers. A VLE might consist of a variety of components designed both to assist in conventional classroom learning as well as support distance learners gaining remote access to an institution's course and assessment materials.
>
> BECTA Virtual and Managed Learning Environments archived April 2005. Available from http://foi.becta.org.uk/display.cfm?resID=15963 [Accessed 3 April 2010].

So VLEs extend teaching and learning, outside the physical classroom. They support the sharing of information and interaction between teachers with their colleagues and teacher with their learners.

Creative arts and media learners need frequent access to computers and the Internet to research and produce work for qualifications and to model industry working practices. If their work is to be produced under controlled conditions (i.e. in the classroom or studio rather than at home) it becomes essential for the educational organization to facilitate Internet access.

Creative arts and media learners need the Internet to:

- Explore creative and media products, for example observe live streaming of concerts, access images from archives and libraries, listen to podcasts, observe programmes
- Research current information relating to the creative industries (e.g. employment figures, job roles)
- Acquire content to use in their creative and media projects (e.g. copyright free music and images)

- Use email to contact industry professionals and organizations, such as a client for whom they may be producing work

- Promote their own work and gain feedback via open access websites such as YouTube and Facebook

- Access interactive learning materials from educational sites (e.g. LSIS Excellence Gateway Creative and media resource).

Links and partnerships with creative arts and media professionals

Partnerships

When learners are asked about their education, what they usually talk about are not the facilities or the equipment but their teachers and their peers. You are the most important resource that your learners have!

Musicians, dancers, actors and artists know that for most people, teach-yourself books or the Internet will never be as effective as the face-to-face demonstration and support they receive from a teacher. You are a valuable resource. But however good you are, you should not be working in isolation.

Partnerships within your organization

It is likely that at some point you will be delivering a programme with other teachers, some of whom may be part-time. It is essential that you spend time on finding out what skills, qualities and experience other people in your team possess. There may be someone in your teaching team who is really good at managing video projects or organizing exhibitions. Another may be an examiner for an awarding body who can offer advice on standards. During initial planning meetings, you should also share the characteristics, needs and expectations of your learner and your understanding of the demands of the intended programme of learning, including summative assessment. Only then can you plan a coherent curriculum and schemes of work that you all feel comfortable with. Regular communication whether face-to-face or via email or a VLE is key to effective working relationships.

If you are the sole person responsible for delivering a programme such as music or art GCSE within your organization, you might consider making links with other music or art teachers in your region.

It is also important to communicate with your line manager on a regular basis. They cannot solve your problems or support you if they do not know about issues. FE colleges, work-based organizations or schools with sixth forms may also have a subject learning coach who can support you in developing your professional and subject skills and handle any challenges you might meet in your teaching. In schools and post-16 organizations, you will also have advanced skills teachers, trainers and lecturers.

Internal verifiers and domain assessors can help you produce effective assignments and help with assessment strategies (see Chapter 7 on Assessment). Teachers can often feel they are expected to perform many roles. However, there are usually experts within your organization that are better prepared to support your learners in areas such as counselling, offering careers advice, and assessing literacy and numeracy needs.

Don't forget one final group of people – your learners. They are not empty vessels when they come to you; they will have great experience as consumers of creative and media products and performances. They will most likely have experience (and some may have considerable expertise) in using a range of digital equipment including video cameras, uploading photographs, word processing, surfing the Internet, creating music. You can also encourage your learners to support each other through the use of team work and peer assessment (see Chapters 4 and 7).

Partnerships external to your organization

Whatever creative arts and media programme you are teaching on, learning will be enhanced by input from creative practitioners.

The following interactive resources provide an extensive range of case studies, video clips, audits and CPD activities on the value of industry links and how to make them.

LSIS Excellence Gateway *Creative Contexts*. Available from: http://tlp.excellence-gateway.org.uk/tlp/cam/resource/tc1/tc1mh01.php [Accessed 3 April 2010].

Diploma support. *Engaging Employers: Creative and Media*. Available from: www.diploma-support.org/resourcesandtools/insidework/ee/CM [Accessed 3 April 2010].

Reflection 6.5

Look at the three lists below. Can you provide examples of when you have introduced this type of resource into your programmes or how you might do this in the future?

Visiting speakers:

- Freelance artists, photographers, musicians, actors, dancers, writers, composers, video makers
- Representatives of companies, such as theatres, recording studio managers, agencies, publishers, hospital radio
- Representatives from regulatory bodies or national organizations, e.g. BBFC, British Film Institute (BFI), Royal Academy.

Visits:

- Guided tours
- Open days
- Audience members, for instance television programmes, theatre performances, art exhibitions.

A client or professional involved in delivery and/or assessment

- Competitions
- Master classes
- Demonstrations
- Industry-led workshops.

Competitions

The creative and media industries are highly competitive. Encouraging your learners to enter competitions can:

- Prepare them for this competitive environment
- Provide a focus for their practical work
- Allow them to gain professional feedback on their work.

There are competitions run each year, by all sorts of different organizations. Which of the examples below have you heard about?

- The Co-operative gives young people aged 19 and under the chance to have their short films shown on the big screen at the prestigious Co-operative Film Festival, formerly known as Co-operative Young Film-Makers.
- The Institute of Mines, Minerals and Manufacturing runs a packaging design competition called Starpack for schools and colleges.
- In 2009, an art competition was run by the Prime Minister's Office which called on 'budding young artists to put pens, pencils and brushes to paper for the Number 10 Art Competition'. Entrants included those between the ages of 12 and 16 and could be painters, sketchers or digital artists. The theme of the competition was the environment.
- UK Skills is a not-for-profit organization. They champion skills and learning for work through the delivery of innovative, high-profile competitions and awards which showcase excellence, and demonstrate how exceptional performance improves individual and organizational success.
- In 2010, the Learning and Skills Improvement Service (LSIS) ran a music competition for learners in post-16 education. The prize was a recording session at Abbey Road Studios in London and a meeting with a top manager.

Funding for resources

Creative arts and media programmes are often expensive in terms of resource provision. However, funds can be found from a variety of sources to pay for equipment, visits or workshops. You, your managers and your learners may be able to contribute to ways to raise finance, for example from grants, charities, lottery money, working for a client, selling tickets for student performances or fashion shows, or setting up an in-house company to make videos or print ephemera.

Planning continuing professional development

CPD and dual professionalism

Creative arts and media teachers are prime examples of people who are dual professionals not only with subject or vocational expertise in art and design, performing arts or media but also with teaching expertise. Continuing professional development (CPD) is the process whereby you can maintain and develop your subject or vocational specialism and the skills and knowledge needed to deliver it effectively. The Institute for Learning requires post-16 teachers to carry out 30 hours (pro rata) of CPD each year. By reading this book, trying the activities and responding to the reflections prompts, you will have completed a significant part of this requirement!

In this chapter, we have concentrated on the range of resources that you can have an influence over. We have steered clear of identifying the best dimensions for a design studio or what constitutes the best mixing desk or lighting grid. These things are often a matter of choice or taste and the discussions are beyond the scope of this book. It is also the case that sometimes the best results can be obtained from the most unlikely situations. Some years ago, one of the authors delivered a performing arts course in an old engineering block. In retrospect this was the best space he ever worked in! However, you should not always have to settle for what you are given and we hope this chapter enables you to explain your resource requirements coherently to a manager so that you can obtain the best possible resources, physical, electronic and human for your learners and yourself.

Useful websites

Institute for Learning: *CPD Guidelines*. Available from: www.ifl.ac.uk/cpd-guidelines [Accessed 3 April 2010].

JISC (Joint Information Systems Committee) (2006) *Designing Spaces for Effective Learning*. Available from: www.jisc.ac.uk/eli_learningspaces.html [Accessed 21 July 2010].

LSIS Excellence Gateway: *Continuing Professional Development*. Available from: http://tlp. excellencegateway.org.uk/tlp/top/professional-development.html [Accessed 3 April 2010].

LSIS Excellence Gateway Teaching and Learning: *Creative and Media*. Available from: http://tlp.excellencegateway.org.uk/tlp/cam/resource/html/resources.php [Accessed 2 April 2010].

Teaching Outside the Classroom is an organization which helps development placements for teachers in settings outside traditional classrooms. Available from: www.teachingoutside-theclassroom.com/home/about-us [Accessed 21 July 2010].

Virtual Learning Environments Becta: *Virtual Learning Environments*. Available from: http://research.becta.org.uk/index.php?section=rh&rid=13640 [Accessed 2 April 2010].

Competitions

Co-operative Film Festival. Available from: http://filmfestival.co-operative.coop/ [Accessed 3 April 2010].

LSIS Excellence Gateway: *Music Competition* and LSIS Excellence Gateway *Music: Enter a Competition*. Available from: http://tlp.excellencegateway.org.uk/tlp/cam/music/competition.aspx [Accessed 3 April 2010].

UK Skills. Available from: www.ukskills.org.uk/about/ [Accessed 3 April 2010].

Institute of Mines, Minerals and Manufacturing. Available from: www.iom3.org/starpack [Accessed 19 April 2010].

Further reading

BECTA (British Educational Communications and Technology Agency) (2006) *ICT and E-Learning in FE*. Coventry: BECTA.

Finlayson, H., Maxwell, B., Caillau, I. and Tomalin, J. (2006) *E-learning in Further Education: The Impact on Student Intermediate and End-point Outcomes*. Sheffield: Centre for Education Research, Sheffield Hallam University.

Hill, C. (2007) *Teaching with E-learning in the Lifelong Learning Sector*, 2nd edn. Exeter: Learning Matters.

Race, P. (2004) *500 Tips for Open and Online Learning*, 4th edn. London: Routledge & Falmer.

7
Assessment

By the end of this chapter, you will be able to:

- Understand the formative and summative assessment of creative arts and media work
- Know what is to be assessed and when, how and by whom
- Enable different types of evidence to be produced by individual creative arts and media learners

Introduction

The assessment of work produced by creative arts and media learners is highly complex. As we noted in Chapter 1, it is hard to explain what is meant by creativity, let alone identify a standard. Consider the following challenges when assessing work:

- What is an original idea?
- How do you compare the level of creativity of an individual author with the creativity of a member of a team producing a computer game?
- Are we in danger of assessing learners' ability to write or talk *about* their creativity and skills rather than their ability to *be* creative or an effective member of a team?
- Does it matter how long or how regularly you practise an instrument or dance if the final performance is excellent?
- Should an artist be penalized if they have not carried out a wide range of primary or secondary research if their ideas and techniques are exciting and original?
- Does the cerebral, fluid nature of creativity get lost in modules or units that offer a formulaic pattern of research, plan, do and evaluate?

Assessment of creativity can be daunting for teachers. What is easier to assess is the individual skill, process or technique involved in creativity and producing creative arts and media products, artefacts or performances and evaluating learners' progress in developing and using these.

In this chapter we look at how effective formative assessment can support learner progression,[1] and how to help learners gain certification for their work. We discuss when it is appropriate to assess learners and how to avoid over-assessment.

The section on summative assessment (pp. 118–20) considers what needs to be assessed in terms of knowledge, understanding and skills; product or process; individual or group work and how assessment is carried out, including the controlled conditions under which learner evidence is produced. The different roles involved in assessment are clarified, such as centre assessor, internal verifier, domain assessor, external examiner and how industry practitioners might be involved in the assessment process.

The use of different types of evidence are explained and how to ensure that this evidence will meet the requirements of specific qualifications. There is a section on how to write assignments that can develop learner skills or meet the assessment criteria for specific qualifications.

Formative and summative assessment of creative arts and media work

Progression

Learner progression was defined by the former Department of Children, Schools and Families as 'An individual learner's progression from engagement in learning to further stages of learning and employment to fulfil personal, professional and/or academic aspirations'.[2]

There is quite rightly a requirement for teachers to ensure that their creative arts and media learners progress and this progression is often measured by their learners' ability to achieve individual qualifications at a certain grade. Awarding bodies, heads of centres, curriculum managers, parents, carers and learners themselves put enormous pressure on teachers to enable their learners to gain certificates and achieve high grades. This may limit delivery to providing the knowledge and skills needed for exams or for final projects rather than on the knowledge and skills that learners need to meet their wider creative and developmental needs. An effective way to address these needs is through the use of formative assessment.

Formative assessment

Formative assessment, sometimes called assessment for learning, is a continuous process that checks learning and gives constructive feedback that encourages further learning. Why is it important?

Used effectively formative assessment means that:

- Teachers do not need to spoon feed information; learners take responsibility for their own learning. They gain confidence in working more independently and making their own decisions. This can help them carrying out lead roles such as producer, choreographer or editor when working on production projects.

- Over-assessment is avoided; learners are able to transfer feedback on one activity or project to another activity, project or work experience and avoid making the same errors.
- Learners feel that they have control and ownership of their learning. This is particularly valuable for creative arts and media learners who are explorative, who want to be seen as individuals (not one of a pack) and may question 'authority'. They can use the knowledge and skills outside the classroom to achieve personal aspirations.

Formative feedback involves the learner in a dialogue in what and how they learn. It is less about tests and worksheets (e.g. identifying the parts of the camera) and more about process (e.g. 'When taking that photograph, why did you choose that setting? Is it helpful to read the camera handbook or do you just need more practice?'). Formative feedback can be written but prompt, informal, face-to-face verbal feedback can have more effect.

There is a focus on developing learners' generic and transferable skills, and their ability to learn and self-assess. For example, if a learner presents a production budget that is unrealistic, formative feedback will do more than identify errors in mathematics or unlikely costs of materials. The teacher will question the learner as to how the budget might be improved, direct the learner to research sources for costings and suggest ways in which they might develop and practise their mathematical skills and which teachers can help them.

Assessment for learning is initially time consuming, particularly if learners are accustomed to less active learning approaches. It is much quicker to give a handout, tell learners facts or demonstrate than allow learners to explore, experiment and practise. However, learners who receive effective formative assessment and as a result become more independent and able to plan, monitor and evaluate their work will achieve more later on in a more time effective way and achieve higher grades, particularly at level 3.

Reflection 7.1

Look at the ten principles of assessment for learning in Table 7.1. Reflect on each of these, look at the examples in the right-hand column and make notes identifying your own examples and the extent to which they are met within your creative arts and media department.

Summative assessment

Summative assessment means that the teacher or an external moderator or examiner will judge learners' creative arts and media knowledge, understanding and skills against standards at specific levels. These judgements are usually made at the end of a unit of work, year or key stage.

Table 7.1 Ten principles of assessment for learning

Principle	Assessment for learning should:	Examples
1	Be part of effective planning of teaching and learning	A creative arts and media session plan that identifies feedback points during and at the end of a session (e.g. team production meetings and question and answer sessions)
2	Focus on how students learn	Ask learners to identify at the end of each session what they have learned (e.g. copyright legislation) and how they have learned (e.g. through debate, case studies, Internet research, talking to an industry professional, copywriting their own material)
3	Be recognized as central to classroom practice	Each session provides opportunity for a range of feedback opportunities; questions and answer sessions on what is to be delivered and the session's activities, peer group feedback on work carried out in the session, periods of quiet reflection for individual learners to reflect on their own contribution to the work and how they might improve it
4	Be regarded as a key professional skill for teachers	Organize or engage in a group or individual continuing professional development (CPD) activity focusing on formative feedback. Feedback on cohorts of learners is regularly shared both formally and informally with other teachers in the team
5	Be sensitive and constructive because any assessment has an emotional impact	A learner hands in their work late – a fashion garment and portfolio. The garment is unimaginative and poorly made; the portfolio is disorganized and has parts missing. The teacher provides the opportunity to explain why there have been problems with the work, listens carefully and reminds the learner of good quality work done previously and the positive personal qualities they have shown in class sessions
6	Take account of the importance of learner motivation	The teacher gives instant feedback when observing a practical activity such as a dance rehearsal that immediately supports an improvement discernible to the learner
7	Promote commitment to learning goals and a shared understanding of the criteria by which they are assessed	The teacher carries out individual or group tutorials before starting a new project and checks that learners understand learning outcomes, the type of evidence they will need to produce, the assessment criteria and the feedback and support they can expect

(Continued overleaf)

Table 7.1 Continued.

Principle	Assessment for learning should:	Examples
8	Give learners constructive guidance about how to improve	The teacher does not give a mark or grade but provides specific advice, e.g. 'You had a great idea for your horror film but a client might expect more evidence of research. Did you think of looking at box office figures to find out which types of horror films were popular? What methods of primary research might you carry out with your peers to find out about popular horror genres?'
9	Develop learners' capacity for self-assessment so that they can become reflective and self-managing	The group critique a famous work of art or perform-ance. They brainstorm the strong points in the work and compile a glossary of 'critical' words. Next session they identify positive critical words and explore how to give constructive and sensitive feedback to their peers. Over time, they work in small groups to practise evaluating some activity or part of an activity they have carried out during the session. They focus on supporting each other in assessing and improving their work.
10	Recognize the full range of achieve-ments of all learners	The teacher in a tutorial does not limit feedback to written work but talks to the learner about other skills they demonstrate inside and outside the classroom, such as a professional attitude, commitment to rehearsal schedules, supporting their production team.

Who is being assessed: needs of learners

During effective recruitment and induction, the abilities, learning preferences and needs of individual learners will have been identified. If they have learning difficulties or physi-cal disabilities, the support they need during their programme may also be needed when they complete a summative assessment. They may require a scribe to record written responses or extra time to complete an exam paper. Awarding organizations will always provide information on the conditions under which summative assessment should take place and what support is appropriate. If the learner's work is assessed through a centre-devised assignment, the teacher writing the assignment should consider what type of evidence would allow individual learners the best opportunity to demonstrate their knowledge or skills. (See the section on pp. 120–7 about types of evidence.)

When to assess: preparing for summative assessment

When the summative assessment takes the form of an examination, this will be at a fixed time. You should build in sufficient time for revision. What is more of an issue is when summative assessment is portfolio based and learners can produce evidence at any time during their programme. This can lead to an 'if it moves – assess it!' approach. There is a clear danger here:

- Candidates will produce work before they have had a chance to develop knowledge and skills.
- Candidates will produce a large volume of work that is a burden for you the teacher to assess, particularly if there are lots of presentations or videos to watch.
- Candidates have difficulty in organizing the work in a coherent fashion.
- Candidates are not producing work independently because they are still being taught.

Reflection 7.2

Look at the assessment readiness checklist in Table 7.2.

- How might you use this checklist when planning your programme?
- What else might you add to the checklist? You could add a third column identifying how and when appropriate actions were taken.

What is being assessed: knowledge, understanding and skills

Many, but not all, creative arts and media qualifications, such as the Diploma in Creative and Media, focus on process rather than the end product. By contrast, an Associated Board Instrumental Examination will focus on a candidate's performance on the day – not how much they practised to achieve the standard or researched the music or composer. Learners should be aware of these differences.

Increasingly there is a requirement for learners to demonstrate that they can follow industry working practices. This often means that they are working in teams. This can present a challenge for the teachers and external moderators and examiners who have to assess individual achievement and grade individual contributions to

Table 7.2 Assessment readiness checklist

Statement	Yes/No
My candidates understand the difference between tasks and activities that will receive formative assessment and evidence that will be produced for summative assessment	
My candidates have had time to gain knowledge and understanding and develop skills to prepare them for summative assessment	
My candidates have been given appropriate formative assessment	
My candidates know the date for an exam or the period when they will be producing evidence for their summative assessment	
I know what formative assessment my learners have received from other teachers (e.g. functional skills teachers) that has prepared them for summative assessment	
My candidates have been given time to revise and/or organize their portfolios	
Other	

group work. This can be addressed by the way in which an assignment is written and the type of evidence that individual learners produce.

Different types of evidence produced by creative arts and media learners

The evidence produced by most creative arts and media learners is rich and varied. As mentioned in the section above about needs of individual learners, the evidence should provide the best opportunities for each candidate to demonstrate their knowledge and skills.

Reflection 7.3

Listed below are different types of evidence produced by creative arts and media candidates. Some strengths are identified for each type as well as suggestions on how they might be best used. As you read this section, reflect on:

- Why your candidates produce some types of evidence more than others – their choice or yours?
- What skills do learners need to produce this evidence – speaking, writing, ICT?
- What other forms of evidence might your learners produce, for example those that use new technology such as podcasts with which they are familiar.

Products, performance and artefacts

Strengths
The end product whether it is a media product, artefact, or performance is usually a main focus and moment of pride for both the learners and you the teacher when after weeks of effort, ideas, planning and practise are all brought to fruition. Producing an end product still remains important, even when processes are being assessed.

Suggestions
Without an end product, the learner cannot get valuable feedback from clients, consumers or audiences that will enable them to evaluate how effective the process has been. Ensure that learners have opportunities to show their work to a target audience and collect feedback through questionnaires, surveys or focus groups.

External moderators may not see the actual performance, artefacts or exhibitions of the work so it is important that other evidence such as video clips or photographs present the quality of the work effectively.

Teacher witness statements and observation reports

Strengths
These can provide useful feedback as part of formative and summative assessment. You are familiar with the learners, the grading criteria and the project assignment. A

few well-chosen words, linking what you see to the grading criteria, can reinforce learner's written evaluations of their contributions to production or performance. You might notice strengths and areas for improvement that learners miss because they are focusing on their role.

Suggestions

You can prepare a list of skills or working practices that you expect to observe and tick these off. Supplement this with some well-chosen comments that directly relate to the individual candidate and that provide examples of an individual learner's skill that justify grading decisions or identify areas for improvement (see Box 7.1). Be very focused on what and who you are observing. An external moderator will not be interested in statements that apply to a whole group.

Industry practitioner witness statements and observation reports

Strengths

Learners really value comments made by industry experts as a result of an industry-linked project or work experience. Learners can quote positive remarks when applying for a university place or a job.

Suggestions

Industry professionals may need direction about what they write. Some might even feel daunted by the thought of writing what they might think is a report. Some may also have literacy problems. You might suggest to them which aspects of the learner's work they should observe, for example attitude, technical skills, creativity, team working, punctuality, research. You might also ask them to identify improvements or areas for development that will help the learner progress.

Box 7.1 Example of what might be included in an observation

The learner:
used a camera	Yes
worked safely	No
worked in a team	Yes

Comments:

You set up and used the camera with some assistance from the technician to take a range of establishing and tracking shots. You were clearly listening to your director when operating the camera and selecting positions to take shots. However, you did not use a cable mat; your team might have tripped over the cable. You need to practise different camera shots using a tripod before tackling the next film project. Aim to take more responsibility and be more independent in setting up equipment and ensuring that you follow safe working practices.

Video and audio

Strengths
Learners can find it refreshing to produce evidence that is an alternative to writing. If the learners carry out the filming, it allows them to develop hands on skills and promotes team working. Such visual or auditory evidence can also be used as a stimulus to encourage peer and self-assessment.

Suggestions
Video and audio evidence can take a long time for an external moderator to view or listen to and if it is a group activity that is filmed, it can be difficult to identify individuals. This means that all videos and audio materials should be clearly labelled and be accompanied by an index which indicates timings and who is doing what in each section. You might ask your learners to edit footage or audio recordings so that they highlight the skills they are demonstrating. You might also add comments (as shown in the right-hand column in Table 7.3) which can be used as a basis for formative or summative assessment.

Essays

Strengths
Within the creative arts and media industries, practitioners seldom write essays. However, essays can provide opportunities for learners to demonstrate in-depth knowledge, explore concepts and issues and develop skills in written communication. Learners understand what is meant by an essay – they will have had practice in writing them at school for a number of years. Some actually welcome writing an extended piece of work that they can do individually.

Suggestions
Support learners in writing essays that have a well-defined structure. An essay should be more than a series of ramblings. It is often helpful to give a word limit. Insist that bibliographic references are correctly identified. Encourage learners to make connections between what they write in essays and their practical work. If there is a more industry relevant way to present information such as a report or presentation – use it.

Reports

Strengths
The ability to write reports is extremely useful in the creative and media industries because much of the work is project based. For example, reports are needed to communicate with a client on market conditions or to report to film backers on production progress.

Suggestions
Reports even more than essays should have a structure, using headings and bullet points and should also show objectivity. There are examples of reports on the sector skills councils' websites.[3]

Table 7.3 Example of an index to video footage

Unit: Performance	Title of video: Physical theatre: 1984		
Assessment focus:	Contributes to the production of a performance		

Time code out or duration of sequence	Description	Roles	Tutor feedback
00.00.10 0'10"	Title sequence Shots of stage set Music	Stage manager: Jaz Singh	Jaz kept to the schedule and made sure that the scenery and props were in place throughout the production.
		Stage hands: Asa Hermann Emma Black	Asa and Emma worked well, but Emma forgot to wear all black clothing and could be seen moving flats during the performance
		Sound: Hattie Bates Lighting: Jude McDowd	Hattie and Jude worked the sound and lighting systems competently and lighting in particular was used creatively
00.05.10 5'0"	Dance set in the prison	Dancers: James Smith Lisa Moore Josh O'Connor	James and Lisa performed competently. They could have used the space better. Josh's performance showed creativity and confidence
00.08.40 3'30"	Whole group on stage: actors and dancers	Narrator: Ella Scozi Actors: Jaime Blanc Kat Hobbs	A confident performance by all, showing great stage presence. Excellent team work
00.12.40 4'00"	Dance duet	Dancers: Harri Morgan Jane Smith	A complex routine with some hesitancy. More practice needed in coordinating moves

Presentations

Strengths
Presentations provide great opportunities for learners to develop the speaking and listening skills needed in formal situations such as when they apply for jobs or work in the creative industries. Making presentations is commonplace in the worlds of marketing and advertising. However, artists, performers and media producers often have to sell their ideas or pitch for new business to a client and being able to make a good presentation is a useful skill. If the presentation is electronic, they can also develop visual skills in presenting printed information and images.

Suggestions

Presentation skills do need to be taught and practised. To communicate effectively with an audience information must be presented in a clear way so that it is assimilated easily and interpreted correctly. It requires the ability to:

- Plan and run an event
- Structure and write the 'script', its main points and speaker's notes
- Speak to a live audience
- Organize time
- Manage different resources including equipment
- Be able to handle the unexpected and deal with new questions and issues confidently as they arise during the presentation.

There are a number of factors to consider when making a presentation:

- Purpose of the presentation, for example to inform, give instructions, pitch an idea
- Type of audience or delegates
- Size of the audience or delegate group
- Where the presentation will take place
- The time and date it will take place
- The formality of the occasion
- What equipment is available.

The slides for any presentation should include:

- Aims and objectives of the presentation
- Summary of what is to be covered in the presentation
- Information in bullet-pointed lists
- Information presented using charts and graphs
- A conclusion
- Contact or support details.

The presentation slides should not give comprehensive coverage of what is said. They should provide a summary of all the information. Good presenters will speak around the slides rather than read from them. When producing the slides, great care should be taken that:

- They follow a logical order.
- They fill but do not run over the allocated time.
- Spelling, punctuation and grammar are correct.

- Not too much information is included.
- An appropriate style and size of font is chosen.

Photographs

Strengths
Nearly all learners are able to produce photographic evidence using a camera, mobile phone or other device such as an iPod. They can show either a finished product or the stages in the process by which it is made. If learners find drawing difficult, for example when producing a storyboard, consider allowing them to use photographs instead.

Suggestions
Encourage learners to take lots of photographs of one subject and select the best. Depending on the purpose of the photographs, they should be presented with either headings or annotations that explain why they were taken and what they show.

Storyboards

Strengths
Storyboards are useful not only for media learners creating a film but also for anyone planning or describing a process. Remember, images can be photographed instead of drawn. If you order a self-assembly furniture flat pack you do not expect an essay – you have a series of pictures with instructions. Why do so many learners still describe what they have done in the form of an essay?

Suggestions
A conventional storyboard encourages linear thinking. Asking learners to place the images out of order to create a different meaning or consequence encourages creativity.

Sample work

Strengths
All creative arts and media learners should have examples of work that they should be proud to use for progression to their next stage of learning or show prospective employers. Sample work might include initial ideas, drawings, maquettes, mood boards, demo CDs, video or audio clips, storyboards, photographs and scripts, as well as final items such as garments or news stories.

Suggestions
Encourage learners to be highly selective and choose a couple of items of work that show they can research, plan, contribute to a production or performance to store in either a paper-cased or electronic portfolio. It might also contain reviews of their work by teachers, audiences or industry practitioners with whom they have worked while on work experience. These examples might be taken from coursework, evidence for qualifications or from activities carried out in their personal life.

Research notes

Strengths
Research is a skill in itself and one that is required by many people working in the creative and media industries.

Suggestions
Make sure that learners are aware of why they are doing research and that their research is focused and achievable. How research notes are presented is also important; they should always be annotated and sources identified. (See Chapter 4 (pp. 64–73) on research methods.)

Diaries, work logs, action plans, minutes of meetings, schedules and risk assessments

Strengths
Entries in diaries, plans, minutes and so on made on a regular basis can build up into an extensive record of how skills or ideas have been developed and how individuals have contributed to team productions or performances. It is acceptable and follows industry working practices for all of the above types of evidence for learners to use a pre-existing proforma.

Suggestions
Build in time at the end of a session in which learners can record what has happened and identify improvements of next steps. Some teacher like to hold team meetings at the beginning of a session so that learners have had a chance to reflect on what has happened previously, review work in progress and plan what they will do in the rest of the session.

Sometimes learners find it tedious to write minutes and these and entries in diaries or action plans can lack detail. This may be because they are uncertain about what to write. You might provide them with headings. You might also consider asking individual learners to take responsibility for recording what happens during a specific session. Then after four sessions ask members of each group to compare and assess the quality of their entries. Do they reflect what happened? Do they recognize the extent to which different roles were carried out?

Paper-based and electronic portfolios

Strengths
A portfolio is an excellent way to bring together a learner's best work, particularly if it is visual work. Increasingly learners are now compiling electronic portfolios that can be accessed by learners, teachers, examiners and moderators.

Suggestions
Encourage learners to separate out materials for assessment from general coursework, especially Internet downloads. Most awarding organizations will accept downloads

as evidence only if they have been annotated and their purpose explained in relation to a project or piece of work. All work that is not a learner's own must be acknowledged. Some specifications also require a research log which will identify when the research was carried out (see Table 7.4).

The contents of portfolios should be well presented; multiple drafts (unless required by an awarding organization) should be avoided. In a paper-based portfolio, visuals such as photographs or drawings that are properly mounted and captioned look professional. All portfolios should contain a contents list or index identifying where different work can be located. This is particularly important if the work is evidence for a qualification. The index should clearly identify where assessment criteria or learning outcomes have been met. It helps considerably if pages are numbered.

Table 7.4 Sample research log on ideas for a horror trailer presentation

Research topic	Source	Date of research
Horror conventions	A Nightmare on Elm Street [DVD] [1984]	9/3/10
Official site of a horror film	http:// www.nightmareonelmstreet.com/	11/3/10
History of horror films	http://en.wikipedia.org/wiki/Horror_film	12/3/10
Examples of horror trailers	http:// www.buried.com/horrortrailers/	13/3/10
How to do titling and add music	Steve Dawkins and Ian Wynd (2010) Video Production, Palgrave Macmillan	16/3/10

How will learners' work be assessed?

In Chapter 2, you were directed to explore a range of qualifications. Some of these will be assessed externally through an exam or series of exams. Others will be assessed internally, within an educational centre through project work (see the section on assignment writing, pp. 130–3). Some, like the Diploma in Creative and Media, will include both internally and externally assessed units.

For internally assessed units, tasks are set and marked within a centre against criteria provided by an awarding body. Samples are then moderated by the awarding body. For externally set units, tasks are set and assessed by the awarding body.

Some exams may require only written work, others such as dance or instrumental qualifications are exclusively practical. However, most vocational and applied creative arts and media qualifications will have a balance of practical and theoretical work.

Regardless of whether a qualification is internally or externally assessed, the learner work is required to meet learning outcomes. Assessment criteria specify the standard at which the learner has met the learning outcomes. This standard within a level is then indicated through a grade or mark.

Who is involved in the assessment process?

Learners

Sometimes those who get ignored in the assessment process are the learners themselves. Learners should be aware of and understand learning outcomes and assessment criteria. They should organize their evidence so that it shows where learning outcomes are met and be encouraged to self-assess the evidence they produce.

Teachers

Teachers are central to the assessment process. You may work independently with colleagues to do the following:

- Designing activities that develop the knowledge and skills needed to meet learning outcomes
- Providing formative assessment
- Writing or adapting assignments
- Assessing evidence for internally assessed units using an awarding body's assessment criteria
- Setting mock exam questions
- Marking mock exam papers.

When submitting learner work for external moderation, it should be clear to the external moderator that the work has been assessed by the centre. This should be indicated through the use of ticks, feedback comments and observation statements.

Internal moderator or domain assessor for the Diploma in Creative and Media

Key elements of the roles of the internal moderator or domain assessor include the following:

- Ensuring that teachers understand the awarding body's assessment requirements and procedures.
- Guiding teachers in writing assessment tasks that are valid, fair, enable learners to achieve the full range of grades and reflect local circumstances and opportunities.
- Guiding you in applying the assessment criteria accurately and consistently.
- Sampling and signing off assessed work, checking that it has been marked and graded using the awarding body's assessment criteria and that appropriate feedback has been given to learners.
- Standardizing assessment within creative and media teaching teams or across creative and media disciplines.

External moderators and external examiners

The external examiner will mark all the work submitted to the awarding organization to be examined and usually the teacher is not expected to have already assessed this work. In contrast, the role of an external moderator is to sample and moderate internally assessed work. They may do this on a visit to a centre or the work may be sent to them. Their role is not to mark the work but to decide whether the centre assessor's decisions are in line with national standards.

Clarity

External moderators may spend as little as ten minutes looking at a portfolio for a unit. They need to be able to locate evidence for each learning outcome quickly. Signposting through the use of an index or sticky notes or annotations is recommended. Sometimes the teacher can get too close to learners' work. Try to look at their evidence with the eyes of a stranger.

Most importantly, clarity is not only about locating evidence, but also about clearly justifying why a particular grade or mark has been given. Centre assessors are expected to write comments that explain their decisions. These comments should link the assessment criteria to examples of individual learner evidence. Centre assessors should avoid writing their own grading criteria or mark each piece of work out of ten but always use those provided by the awarding body, even for practice assignments or papers.

Consistency

External moderators are able to allow some tolerance within a batch they are sampling. If a whole batch of work is marked too high or too low, they can adjust marks accordingly. There is more of a problem when a teacher is inconsistent and marks two or three students too harshly or too generously. For example, if five learners marked at merit deserve only a pass but two of the learners graded merit deserve a distinction, the better students may find themselves penalized. All learners with a merit grade may end up with a pass grade.

Collaboration

It is especially important that for new qualifications and those that cover a number of creative arts and media sectors or specialist creative arts and media areas that teachers work with co-deliverers and internal moderators on assessment processes. It is also essential that they attend training from awarding organizations and read the chief examiners' or moderators' reports as well as look at exemplar assessed work which can be found on awarding organizations' websites. Rigorous internal standardization process is key to success and sufficient time should be taken for this process to be carried out prior to submitting marks. Remember – external moderators work together in order to share understanding of levels and grades. They will work in teams and be able to call for advice on specialist areas. They also have the benefit of looking at hundreds of scripts and portfolios from around the country. You too should not work in isolation. Assessment is complex and you need support.

Assignment writing

Assignments are not only for summative assessment but also for developing learners' knowledge and skills. The assignment might cover a whole project, such as producing a theatrical performance, or they may address a discrete task, for instance carrying out a location recce for location filming. An assignment that starts with an industry-based scenario makes the work relevant to the learner and enables them to follow industry working practices in response.

Reflection 7.4

Look at these two examples of scenarios. Think about a scenario that could be used for your learners.

1   You work as a designer for CoolBrat Garments. A retail store wants a new line of childrenswear for next autumn that is environmentally friendly and encourages children to play outdoors. Your boss has asked you to come up with five ideas for boys' coats and source suitable fabrics to show the client. You will show your work in a presentation to the client in three weeks' time. They will expect you to explain why your ideas are appropriate for the current market in childrenswear and see costings for producing the garments.

2   You are a freelance photographer. Create an electronic portfolio of ten photographs that you can sell to the local newspaper which showcase the local environment or a local event. You have one week to complete this work and email the photographs to the editor. You should also suggest a fee for publishing one of the photographs.

The assignment-writing process

A good assignment brief (sometimes called an assessment vehicle) provides learners with opportunities to demonstrate their individual knowledge and skills assignments and facilitates assessment.

It takes a substantial amount of time to write an effective assignment. But a well-written assignment will save time later on when you come to assess the learner work. More importantly, a well-written assignment directs the learner to providing evidence that demonstrates their strengths and enables them to achieve high grades.

Look at the six stages below which guide you through the writing process needed to produce an assignment for summative evidence.

Stage 1: Read the specification
It can be tempting to use an assignment off your shelf that was designed for another qualification and try to tweak it! Check that you understand the learning outcomes or objectives, the assessment criteria and the type of evidence required by the awarding body. If you are unsure about any of these, contact the awarding body.

Stage 2: Explore any model assignments
If this is the first time you have delivered this qualification, then use, adapt or contextualize exemplar assignments. They are useful for suggesting the quantity of

evidence expected and the level of support you can offer learners in completing the assignment.

Stage 3: Write a draft assignment

If you are not using a model assignment, be prepared to draft and redraft the assignment.

Stage 4: Check the draft assignment

Use an assignment checklist (see the example in Table 7.5) to check the quality of your assignment.

Table 7.5 Assignment writing checklist

Question	Examples of comments
1 Is this assignment part of formative or summative assessment?	Formative assessment: Music technology Working title: *Music to Scream For*. Learners are asked to work in small groups to produce a 15-second piece of music to include in a horror film trailer. This is a short project that allows them to practise skills needed for summative assessment
2 Is the assignment a model assignment or an adaptation of a model assignment?	Adapts and shortens a model assignment
3 Is this an integrated assignment? Are there links to other units?	The assignment links to the video production unit
4 Does the assignment cover all learning outcomes or assessment criteria for a unit or module or only some? Is this made explicit?	Learning outcomes 1, 2 and 3: research, plan and produce Outcomes listed below the opening scenario
5 Is the assignment structured in stages that match the learning outcomes or assessment criteria?	Three stages: each stage matches a learning outcome. Stage 1 is divided into tasks: primary research, secondary research, analysis and conclusions drawn from research. Stage 2 tasks include meetings with the client, producing ideas for the music, producing a schedule and budget, carrying out a risk assessment for the studio, monitoring progress. Stage 3 requires them to produce the music to present to a focus group that includes their 'client' and their peers. The tasks are linked to the grading criteria
6 Is there a timescale for each stage? Are learners made aware of whether they can or cannot expect formative feedback at the end of each stage?	Learners will have three sessions to complete each stage. Learners will get verbal feedback throughout the mini-project. There will be written feedback at the end

(Continued overleaf)

Table 7.5 Continued.

Question	Examples of comments
7 Has the assignment an industry scenario, industry brief or a local context? Do the tasks encourage industry working practices?	The teacher will act as a horror film director commissioning the music. Learners will pitch their research and ideas to this client using an electronic presentation
8 Are the tasks clear, using language appropriate for the level of learner? Do the tasks use creative and media terminology?	The language used has been run through a Simple Measure of Gobbledegook (SMOG) test.[4] Learners will have prior knowledge of the music and film terminology used in the assignment such as sampling and music sound spotting
9 Have the learners developed the skills needed to complete the assignment?	Learners have developed research and music composition skills but this project enables them to work in a group to meet a deadline and practise presentation skills.
10 Do the tasks guide the learner towards achieving higher grades or mark bands? Do the tasks ask for more evidence than required by the specification?	The tasks relate to the distinction grade. There is an additional task to challenge learners with video editing skills. They will dub music to an extract of a horror film trailer
11 Is it clear what evidence is required from the learner, such as written or verbal evidence? Does the type of evidence support learners with different needs? Will learners be clear about how to organize the evidence?	Learners can produce either an electronic or paper-based research, planning and production log. The music can be either a recording of a live performance or be created electronically. The assignment includes instructions for learners on how to store their music on the college intranet
12 Does the assignment clarify how learners can produce evidence of individual contributions to group activities?	Learners must identify their contributions in their individual research, planning and production logs
13 Do learners know about any controlled conditions under which they must complete the assignment?	Learners must meet the deadline but can ask for support from teachers and technicians at any time
14 Are learners aware of what resources they can use?	The assignment indicates when learners will have access to laptops with Internet access, music rehearsal rooms and recording equipment

Stage 5: Internally verify the assignment

You should ask an internal verifier within your organization or a line manager to carry out a check. However, it is essential that they understand the requirements of the qualification the assignment is written for. A diploma domain assessor will be an expert in the creative arts and media line of learning.

Stage 6: Produce the final copy of your assignment

Remember to carry out a final check of spelling and grammar.

Reflection 7.5

Look at the checklist in Table 7.5. Reflect on:

- How the checklist can ensure learner achievement
- What other aspects you might want to check.

You could replace the comments column with a Yes/No/Sometimes column.

Assessment is a complex process and one that should be a team effort rather than a solitary process. There should always be people within your organization and external to your organization who can support you in developing an effective assessment process. The big challenge is to provide assessment opportunities for learners that reflect the rapidly changing world of the creative and media industries.

References

1   Formative Assessment. Available from: www.excellencegateway.org.uk/page.aspx?o= 128831 [Accessed 24 July 2010].

2   DCSF (2008) document quoted by LSIS Excellence Gateway in *Supporting Learner Progression* resource. Available from http://tlp.excellencegateway.org.uk/tlp/progression/ aboutprogress/index.html [Accessed 11 October 2010].

3   Example of report: *Staying Ahead: The Economic Performance of the UK's Creative Industries.* Available from: www.creative-choices.co.uk/upload/pdf/20080414_sb_sr_stayingahead. pdf [Accessed 23 July 2010].

4   SMOG (Simple Measure of Gobbledegook). Downloadable booklet available from: http://shop.niace.org.uk/media/catalog/product/R/e/Readability.pdf [Accessed 23 July 2010].

Useful website

Ofqual Office of Qualifications and Examinations Regulation. Available from: http://ofqual. gov.uk/ [Accessed 23 July 2010].

Further reading

Angelo, T. and Cross, P. (1993) *Classroom Assessment Techniques*, 2nd edn. San Francisco, CA: Jossey-Bass.

Armitage, A. and Renwick, A. (2008) *Assessment in FE*. London: Continuum.

Black, P., Harrison, C., Lee, C., Marshall, B. and William, D. (2003) *Assessment for Learning: Putting It into Practice*. Maidenhead: Open University Press.

Cox, A. and Harper, H. (2000) *Planning, Teaching and Assessing Learning: A Reader*. Greenwich: University of Greenwich.

Ecclestone, K. (2003) *Understanding Assessment and Qualifications in Post-Compulsory Education*. Leicester: NIACE.

Gravells, A. (2009) *Principles and Practice of Assessment in the LLL Sector*. Exeter: Learning Matters.

Rowntree, D. (1987) *Assessing Students: How Shall We Know Them?* London: Kogan Page.

Tummons, J. (2007) *Assessing Learning in the Lifelong Learning Sector*, 2nd edn. Exeter: Learning Matters.

Index

BEHAVIOUR IN SCHOOLS 2/E

Louise Porter

9780335220014 (Paperback)
2006

Behaviour management in the classroom and playground is one of the most challenging aspects of teaching. The new edition of *Behaviour in Schools* offers a comprehensive overview of the major theories of behaviour management in primary and secondary schools, illustrated with detailed case studies.

The theories covered include:

- Assertive discipline
- Applied behaviour analysis
- New cognitive behavioural approaches
- Neo-Adlerian theory
- Humanism
- Glasser's control theory
- Systems theory

Maintaining the balance of theory and practice, the new edition has been fully updated in light of recent research, including a strengthened discussion of inclusion and anti-bias curricula, and sections on motivation and self-esteem. References have been also been updated, making fuller use of UK research.

www.openup.co.uk

OPEN UNIVERSITY PRESS
McGraw - Hill Education

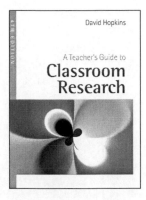

A TEACHER'S GUIDE TO CLASSROOM RESEARCH 4/E

David Hopkins

978-0-335-22174-5 (Paperback)
2008

The fourth edition of this bestselling book is a practical guide for teachers that wish to conduct research in their classrooms and for schools that wish to improve their practice. Classroom research, as described in this book, will enable teachers to enhance their own or their colleagues' teaching, to test the assumptions of educational theory in practice and to implement and evaluate whole school developments.

Changes to the new edition include:

- A major re-working of the last four chapters
- Comprehensive description of how to conduct classroom research
- Two new chapters on analyzing and reporting research
- Updated case study examples and cameos
- The contribution of teacher research in enhancing personalized learning and school transformation

www.openup.co.uk

OPEN UNIVERSITY PRESS
McGraw - Hill Education

APPROACHES TO LEARNING
A Guide for Teachers

Anne Jordan, Orison Carlile
and Annetta Stack

978-0-335-22670-2 (Paperback)
2008

This comprehensive guide for education students and practitioners
provides an overview of the major theories of learning. It considers
their implications for policy and practice and sets out practical
guidelines for best pedagogical practice. This book includes
theoretical perspectives drawn from the philosophy, psychology,
sociology and pedagogy that guide educational principles and
practice.

Each chapter contains:

- A summary of key principles
- Examples and illustrations from contemporary research and
  practice
- Summary boxes that highlight critical and key points made
- Practical implications for education professionals

Approaches to Learning is an invaluable resource for students and
practitioners who wish to reflect on their educational constructs and
explore and engage in the modern discourse of education.

www.openup.co.uk

 OPEN UNIVERSITY PRESS
McGraw - Hill Education